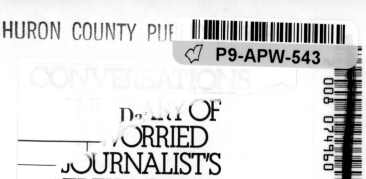

CONVERSATIONS

DIARY OF
A WORRIED
JOURNALIST'S
TREK ACROSS
A DIVIDED
& THREATENED
CANADA

CONVERSATIONS
THE DIARY OF A WORRIED JOURNALIST'S TREK ACROSS A DIVIDED & THREATENED CANADA

JOHN AITKEN

PRENTICE-HALL OF CANADA, LTD.   SCARBOROUGH, ONTARIO

Canadian Cataloguing in Publication Data

Aitken, John, 1936-
  Conversations : the diary of a worried
journalist's trek across a divided and threatened
Canada

ISBN 0-13-172056-2

1. Nationalism-Canada-- Public opinion.
2. Public opinion--Canada.   3. Canada-Politics
and government-1963-   * I. Title.

FC98.A38   971.06'44   C78-001130-9
F1027.A38

Prentice-Hall, Inc., Englewood Cliffs, New Jersey
Prentice-Hall International, Inc., London
Prentice-Hall of Australia, Pty., Ltd., Sydney
Prentice-Hall of India, Pvt., Ltd., New Delhi
Prentice-Hall of Japan, Inc., Tokyo
Prentice-Hall of Southeast Asia (Pte.) Ltd., Singapore

ISBN 0-13-172056-2

Design: Julian Cleva
Cover: William Fox/Associates
Composition: BCS

1 2 3 4 5 JD 82 81 80 79 78

Contents

For Helen

PREAMBLE
Shut up and Listen

THERE'S A lot to be said for traveling long distances by bus. It's cheap, and you don't have to drive.

It's also exhausting, boring, uncomfortable and interminable: at best you can only hope to average 45 miles an hour. You pray that God will protect you from your enemies: fat people, drunks, mothers with squalling brats that need their diapers changed, lunch stops equipped with little more than bubble gum dispensers and Coke machines, lavatory cubicles where graffiti have been applied to the walls with human feces. Above all you pray that the air conditioning works and that when you finally do hole up for a few hours in a second rate hotel the shower will work.

So why, you might ask, have I traveled close to ten thousand miles by bus in the last seven or eight years, especially when someone else was paying and I could have gone by jet complete with first run films, stereophonic music, decent food and bar service?

And I'd have to admit that traveling by bus is fun, once you adapt to the more spartan conditions. And I'd also have to say that it's a way to meet real people, to eavesdrop, to absorb their prejudices and preoccupations, to learn about their real concerns without having them filtered through the media, slickly packaged, synthesized and sterilized, and ultimately

1

pronounced fit for mass consumption by some desk-bound editor in Toronto. Travel by bus and you get raw material, undigested and sometimes unpleasant but always perceived truth; people tend to say what they think. It may be bigoted or beautiful, lunatic, wrong-headed but real; it will be *their* truth, what they'll act upon, what they'll base their votes on. For a journalist, that kind of reality is hard to come by.

This isn't a scientific sampling or opinion poll and I make no pretence of balance in what follows. These were simply conversations I had, over a period of six weeks in the summer of 1977 with people I chanced to meet, or with people I'd heard of and sought out because I thought they might tell me something, give me some insight into their attitudes, their dreams and their despairs. Nor was I primarily concerned with "grass roots" or "silent majority" philosophy, although I would hear a good deal about both.

Bus travel is democratic: there is variety and rhythm to the people you're thrown in with, and they will often share a moment of their lives with you, tell you something about themselves.

Nor are you limited to your fellow travelers. You can get off and explore wherever you please; there'll be another bus along later and maybe that one will have air conditioning that works. Meanwhile you can talk to the town mayor or the town drunk — you'll probably learn something worthwhile from both of them. Or listen, as I did one Sunday morning in Kamloops, to Flying Phil Gaglardi, one-time flamboyant British Columbia highways minister now retired from political life, delivering a sermon on women's liberation at his Calvary Church there. God has an important role for women, he intoned with deep conviction, ". . . in their places." And the good matrons of Kamloops tittered quietly. "The good die young," the Reverend Mr. Gaglardi said, "because it's the men who have the heart attacks." It wasn't the main service; he was giving a sort of fireside chat, interspersed with prayers, to the parents of children attending Sunday School in the church basement and when this mini-service was over I left the building, heading for a park I'd noticed earlier. I was about a block away when an elderly, splendidly dressed woman stopped me on the street. "Oh!" she said with genuine dismay, "you're heading in the wrong direction. You should be coming to Calvary Church."

"I've just come from there," I said. "I heard a sermon by Mr. Gaglardi."

"Oh, but that's not the main service," she said. "Have you been saved?"

"I'm working on it," I said, and we passed each other with friendly smiles. Perhaps mine was more of a rictus than a smile, but a *friendly* rictus nonetheless.

Of course I didn't spend five weeks traveling five thousand miles from Victoria, British Columbia, to St. John's, Newfoundland, to hear an ex-politician's sermon in Kamloops. I did it because of a deep conviction that Canada, for the first time in her brief history, faces a serious threat to her continued existence as a nation. This has been forced on the public consciousness by the election and subsequent actions of Premier René Lévesque, and polarized even further by the controversial Quebec Language Act, which established a precedent that the other provinces will find hard to swallow. Since Lévesque's victory there has been much agonizing, much panic-stricken and ill-considered publicity over the possible, probable or even inevitable secession of Quebec and the disastrous implications this would have for the rest of Canada. Few people seem to have grasped the fact that if, as seems quite possible, Canada fails, René Lévesque will have been but a single factor, a catalyst, in the dissolution of a country that was geographically, politically and economically preposterous from the start.

We are faced with far more serious problems than the current mood — transient and changeable — of a relatively small group of true separatists in Quebec. We have economic chaos clearly beyond the control, let alone the comprehension, of anyone in Ottawa. We have become one of the most strike-happy nations in the Western World. Our true unemployment runs well over a million, yet our insatiable demands for higher and higher standards of living have created unprecedented inflation which, combined with our increasing trade deficit, may well lead to another Depression.

Nor are the Péquistes in Quebec the only "separatists" in Canada. There's a strong and ugly backlash against the French in Ontario (the Essex County school hassle was a single example). Western alienation has become a political cliché; British Columbians have more in common with Seattle and Tokyo than St. John's; the people of the prairie provinces despise Ontario as much as Quebec, some of them more so, for they can identify with Quebec in feeling isolated, exploited, and ignored. Ukrainians of pioneer stock in Manitoba are as impatient with the bilingual demands of Quebec as are the Italians who comprise approximately ten per cent of Toronto's population. French-speaking Canadians in Acadia feel isolated and fear for the future — Lévesque himself has said that the only place for French-speaking Canadians is in Quebec, thus ignoring roots as deep if not deeper than his own. Maritimers believe they've been sold out by Confederation, bankrupted and ignored. A Nova Scotian friend (who was born in British Columbia) tells me his neighbors think the Maritimes could form a nation at least as viable as Norway. If they could entice Newfoundland and Labrador into economic or national union they'd have everything they need — industry, resources, energy, deepwater ports, leadership — to become a thriving and powerful trading nation.

None of this means Canada is doomed, but we *are* being forced to examine our attitudes. Culturally and economically we are dominated by the United States to the point where one must consider what it means to be Canadian, what it *costs* to be Canadian, and whether it's worth it. We have a vast land we can't afford to develop, so we let the Americans do it for us, bitching constantly about the obvious and predictable result: they own our industries and, in English Canada, our minds. First there was Hollywood, then television and most of what we read, and ultimately a massive influx of American teachers dominating campus after campus. Every year we become less Canadian, more American, our allegiance to the British crown a rapidly fading memory. We maintain an ineffectual military force that we can ill afford while any fool knows that in time of war it would be our mighty neighbor who would have to protect us. We spend huge sums of money on welfare and industrial development programs that don't work, in a vain effort to pretend that our country is economically balanced. Building a single pipeline would have bankrupted us, and yet we depend more heavily than the Americans on fuel which is fast running out. Our newspapers ridicule the Prime Minister every time he goes to Washington to bargain — plead, perhaps — for more trade, more manufacturing, more control over our own affairs, our own destiny. The irony is that the Americans don't want us or our land; they just want our resources, and they generally get them.

What, then, is the purpose of continually shoring up a disunited country? What does it mean to *me* when I tell a British inn-keeper "No, I'm not an American, I'm a Canadian." It certainly means damned little to him. He doesn't regard me as a British subject and I don't feel like one either; I'm an American subject and I don't like it a bit, but what can I do about it? Nor do I consider myself anti-American, and if that sounds confused it's because I think there's a great deal of confusion in Canada today.

Ever since the spring of 1971, when I took a four thousand mile bus tour through the United States from Washington, D.C., down through the deep south to New Orleans, then up through the midwest, I've wanted to do something similar in Canada. I'd been Washington correspondent for the *Toronto Telegram* for three years, from 1967 to 1970, and during that period I logged some fifty thousand miles covering assassination aftermaths, riots, space shots, politics, peace movements and anything else that came along; I visited about 35 states, maybe 38, and it was exciting and rewarding, often thrilling work. It was also the time in my life when I began to *feel* Canadian, to *think* Canadian, despite the fact that I was born in Toronto. Until then I'd never given the matter much thought.

But despite the travel and excitement, I had seen little of the United States. Mostly I'd seen airports and hotel rooms and an awful lot of sky; the view from forty thousand feet is limited, and contact with the mass of people was nil. Hence the first bus tour, which gave me insights that I treasure — a sense of the vastness of the land. I had spent the years in Washington almost exclusively in the company of politicians, bureaucrats, diplomats and, inevitably, other Canadian journalists. Traveling by bus I met many of the ordinary people of the land and I learned much from them.

Another thing: although I'd been to the east coast several times, both as a child and on assignments as a newspaper reporter, I had never been west of Sarnia in Canada. Thus my second bus tour became an obsession, simply a matter of time: finding someone who would believe in it and finance it. Meanwhile I contrived to do articles which would take me to places in Canada where I hadn't been and in this I was fairly successful. I was able to visit all the provinces but Newfoundland and Prince Edward Island (where I vacationed as a child). I've been to the Yukon, the Northwest Territories and the Quebec side of James Bay. I criss-crossed Canada for several years, still at forty thousand feet, but at least seeing pockets of Canada, meeting handfuls of her people, sensing some of the distances, the variety and fragility of taiga and tundra, prairies and Rockies. Life was a picnic and journalism the price of admission and no one expected you to take it all seriously.

That's all changed now. When René Lévesque was elected, and perhaps for a while before that, I began to feel that I was getting more interpretation than information, more punditry than reality; everything I read or heard was second-hand and I mistrusted it. I wanted to get out into the country again, at ground level, and hear what people were talking about, feel, if I could, what they felt. We Torontonians live in splendid isolation, secure among our millions of people, our mushrooming highrises, a proliferation of expensive and occasionally quite good places to dine, a subway that works, boutiques and body rubs and something we call sophistication. But often I'll go downtown and gawk at the skyscrapers, each with a daytime population equivalent to a small town, and the absurdity of Toronto hits me: we are a mighty city dominating the affairs of the nation, and what are all the people in those skyscrapers doing? They're shuffling papers from one side of their desks to the other seven hours a day, five days a week, forty-nine or fifty weeks a year. We are a decadent satellite and totally unreal.

That is why it was time to hop on a bus for a few weeks. I wasn't looking for answers or even truth, but merely reality. I wanted to know if what people were saying was as scary as the stuff I was reading in the newspapers. To a certain extent it was, but leavened, usually, with a wry sense of humor which I found reassuring. Sometimes I found solace in my own sense of the ridiculous. Sometimes it was excruciatingly lonely and depressing and there were moments of outrage and anger. But there were other times when I felt a sense of grandeur and power and even tranquility and hope. And of course there were the people. They were seldom dull.

There's a pin-stripey, gun-totin' millionaire lawyer in Calgary who keeps a Walther PPK double action pistol in his right-hand pants' pocket (fully loaded clip and a cartridge up the spout just to be sure), a Colt revolver magnetized to his desk and God knows what he's got in his glove compartment or tucked away at home. He wants — *intends* — the Province of Alberta to be declared a sovereign nation state in less than two years and he may be nuts but he sure isn't crazy. And I met a black political scientist from Toronto (she came from the Caribbean twenty years ago) on a bus in Fredericton and she neither knew nor seemed to care about the disastrous (and deserved) Davis election results in Ontario a day or two before. When I observed that a political scientist less than a thesis away from her Ph.D. might reasonably be expected to have at least a passing interest in politics she got quietly angry and told me she figures that sometime in the next thirty years white America is going to get exasperated and murder twenty million blacks — pure Hitlerian genocide, but on a much grander scale — and that she found it difficult to take Ottawa, much less Queen's Park, seriously. She, it appears, distinguishes between the abstract and absorbing discipline of political science and the hurly-burly world of politics. Politics is never abstract; it's a rough, dirty game with few rules and elastic ethics. Political science, I think, is rarely exciting and I suppose the black people have had sufficient excitement in the past three hundred years.

There were a couple of twenty-year-olds on the way to North Sydney who were drinking beer, smoking marijuana and comparing prison records. Both of them were heavily and inexpertly tattooed with such epithets as "loser" and "FTW" which stands for "Fuck The World" and one of them had a really nasty gash on his finger, straddling the knuckle. He'd been at a lease-breaking party for a friend in Halifax, he said, and he'd been smashing windows bare-handed. The cut should have had at least a dozen stitches but he'd passed out shortly after it happened and said he was too drunk to go to the hospital.

I met a man who grows wheat just for the fun of it near Regina and as a hobby it sounded almost as expensive as maintaining a mistress. I mean he'd already spent $1,100 on chemicals alone! And in Vancouver an amiably sodden young man struck up a slurred but reasonably coherent conversation, asking how things were in Toronto and what I was doing in Vancouver. He'd seen me jotting things down in my notebook so I couldn't tell him I was a tourist or selling computer software or some such thing.

"Well," I said, wishing I could think of something else to say, "I'm writing a book." It was an explanation I had to give many times in the next few weeks and I never felt comfortable with it, partly because it tends to frighten people off. They think you're going to write about *them*, which of course you are. And then they'd ask what the book was about and I couldn't really answer that one very satisfactorily. I wouldn't really know myself until it was written. People, certainly, the people I'd meet on my five-thousand-mile odyssey. Politics to some extent, because of the great upheavals threatening Canada today, but not primarily politicians. They talk too much and say too little.

I just wanted to *listen* to people — accidental people who would happen to me along the way. Like, Marie, the spare change girl in Vancouver who was more than a panhandler, and the two young men with their hopelessness tattooed on their forearms, and the man who was bicycling from the Queen Charlotte Islands eighty-five miles off the coast of northern British Columbia, to Windsor, three thousand miles or more east. And the separatists and the don't-give-a-damns who scramble for jobs that don't exist or settle back and collect welfare cheques. I wasn't looking for important people and I had few questions to ask. I thought I'd learn more just by listening.

Jim McNiven, for example, the executive director of the Atlantic Provinces Economic Council in Halifax, told me: "If there's anything distinctive about Canadians it's their ability to divide themselves into ever smaller groups." And that was the point of the exercise: it is this conglomeration of people, their attitudes and prejudices, apathies and hungers, with whom my future and Canada's are inextricably linked, and I wanted to know them better.

So when people asked what my book would be about I'd say "Politics, mostly," and that reassured them. After all, what did *they* have to do with *politics*?

BRITISH COLUMBIA
Socialism, Separatism and Seattle

Marie, THE spare change girl from Nova Scotia someplace, hasn't met Doug Christie and neither had I when I encountered her in Vancouver so I don't know what she'd have thought of his scheme to make her a millionaire. I doubt if she'd have been much impressed and anyway Christie's a pretty conservative guy; if he'd met her he might have changed his mind.

We used to call people like Marie hippies, flower children who bravely protested against other countries' wars and injustices, but that's almost a generation ago now. Marie was a panhandler, patrolling Vancouver's Granville Street mall on a balmy evening. She approached people with a puppy dog smile and she'd singsong a forlorn little "got-any-spare-change-thank-you" seeming oblivious to the fact that nobody gave her a penny. I watched her for a few minutes, wondering why I was doing so. I had just flown in from Toronto, a long, boring flight, checked in at the Sylvia Hotel on English Bay and strolled over to the mall to find a quiet place in which to reflect on the madness of my endeavor, and there I was, lounging instead against somebody's store window, hypnotized by a grimy waif with dirty feet and stringy hair and a figure hardly worth a glance. A nothing kid. A panhandler.

She spotted me and weaved through the stream of people. "Got-any-spare-change-thank-you" and I shook my head. I'd given my last quarter to a disgruntled airport cab driver. Spare bills I did have, and maybe she saw some flicker of deceit for she stopped and looked me in the eye. "Throw a quarter and I'll run for it," she said earnestly. "I really did that for a guy once." So I gave her a dollar and said "C'mon, I'll buy you a hamburger," but she said no, she had to keep working, this was her peak period, and that's when it came to me: she *enjoyed* what she was doing. She was even proud of herself. I asked where she came from and she said "Nova-Scotia-someplace."

"Long way from home," I said with middle-aged sagacity. "What are you doing here?"

"Panhandling," she said, but she wasn't being sarcastic, just surprised that I hadn't noticed. There was a group of them, she said, camped on one of the beaches nearby. They hadn't been in town long enough for welfare, none of them had found a job yet and it was her turn to forage for the others. She figured she'd make ten dollars, she said. "Maybe even twenty on a really good night." She'd already raised seven dollars, the sun hadn't set and it was early.

I met her again at about eleven o'clock and asked how she'd done in the four or five hours that had passed. "Five dollars," she said. "I made five dollars."

"Last time you told me you'd already made seven," I said, immediately regretting it. It had not, after all, been a good night.

"I counted wrong," she said firmly. "I only made five." She turned toward an approaching denim-clad couple, smile in place, chanting "Got-any-spare-change-thank-you" as they drifted past her into the night.

Douglas H. CHRISTIE, a 32-year-old barrister and solicitor in Victoria, B.C., is founder and chairman of the Committee for Western Independence and he is dedicated to the destruction of Canada. He doesn't see it that way, of course; I do.

Christie sounded like an excited schoolboy when I called his Victoria law office the next morning. I was telephoning from Vancouver to make an appointment to see him; I'd already told his secretary who I was and what I wanted and he was prepared for me. He'd just had this terrific idea, he said. "The Americans want a pipeline to Alaska and they don't particularly want it on Canadian soil, and British Columbia gets no great benefit from Confederation, so we'll offer British Columbia to the United States for $26 billion — that'd mean a million dollars for every British Columbian."

"Well, it sure beats panhandling," I said, but I don't think he heard me and anyway his arithmetic was wrong. It only works out to about $10,000, hardly enough for the down payment on a house. I guess he was being a bit smart-ass with the eastern writer, putting me in my place. I was just as bad; I'd already written him off, prematurely and inaccurately, as part of the Lotus Land lunatic fringe. He and Marie were among the first people I met in British Columbia and they seemed to complement each other in a frightening sort of way, the one devoting himself to the destruction of a country, the other virtually ignoring its existence, and both of them, like it or not, my fellow citizens: Canadians to a fault.

Christie, when I arrived in Victoria to see him the following day, sat in his cramped Fort Street office glowering, and told me that "Western Canada has no substantial future in Confederation." Finally I had confronted the enemy: an anglophone separatist. Interview hell, I was boiling for battle! But my sense of outraged indignation didn't last very long. Christie isn't western separatist, he's just a chauvinistic British Columbian activist with a bent for melodrama and demagoguery. Sincere, mind you.

"Independence," he told me, "is something that can be

attained within or without Confederation. We haven't abandoned the possibilities of accommodation but we're pessimistic . . . We just don't feel that Confederation will ever give Western Canada a means of attaining its economic, cultural, linguistic or social fulfillment.''

Now you have to understand there are several "Western Canadas" and he was referring to just one of them, perhaps two at most. British Columbians, justifiably enough, regard themselves as westerners, although colloquially and because of the Rocky Mountains, they're more accurately west coasters, part of a geographic community that extends through Seattle, San Francisco and Los Angeles. Economically they're part of the Pacific Rim complex of nations which includes Australia and Japan. Prairie farmers think Western Canada begins at the Ontario border and ends at the foothills of the Rockies and the rest of us think of Western Canada as anything to the left of us, or as British Columbia and the prairies combined. It's a little confusing sometimes.

Doug Christie is a British Columbian by adoption, with roots in Western Canada (he graduated from the University of Winnipeg 1967, then travelled to Vancouver for law school, spending his summers working in Alberta) but is, after seven years of law practice, almost a *parvenu* by Victorian standards. No matter; he *is* a westerner.

When he refers to economics, language, culture and social fulfillment he's talking about money and jobs, the central preoccupations of most adult Canadians today regardless of what language they speak or how red the skin on the backs of their necks. The economy — unemployment and inflation — is Canada's primary crisis today, with national unity a sort of inter-related close second. These two themes may get twisted about in the next election or two because we no longer believe the myth that any individual government can do very much about the economy, while the question of national unity is newer to us, more emotionally charged and dramatic and would make a more satisfying — if hopelessly irrelevant — election issue.

Joblessness in British Columbia, at time of writing, runs

officially at about 8.5 per cent, down a little from a year ago but since the labor force rose by about 30,000 during that year the actual number of unemployed is higher. I was told that the jobless figures range up to 30 per cent in the construction industry and maybe as high as 36 per cent among carpenters (if you discount the odd bit of home-fix-it moonlighting). That's not as high as Newfoundland's 17 per cent unemployment rate (Oh, all right, it can go as high as 55 per cent in some Newfoundland communities and some northern Ontario ones, too!) but it's high enough to bring out some fairly typical West Coast hostilities.

Freighters arrive from Japan, their cargo holds filled with trainloads of Datsuns, Hondas and Toyotas which cost a British Columbian buyer about $600 more than they'd cost in Seattle or San Francisco. That's because of the auto pact we made [in 1965] with President Johnson. We'd tax "foreign" cars if Detroit would let us assemble American cars, which means lots of well-paid automotive industry jobs in Oakville and Oshawa. That doesn't cut much ice with British Columbians who don't really believe easterners know they exist. And anyway, the pact has failed. In 1975 our auto trade deficit with the U.S. reached $1.9 billion. Christie claims flatly that "our economic interests here are not with Confederation but with resources located here, and trade with the Pacific Rim countries — Japan, Australia — and with the western United States. If we could trade with coastal states as equals and not as subservients of the economic interests of central Canada, if we were able to buy on the world market what we cannot manufacture, at world market prices rather than tariff-protected prices, our standard of living would be 30 per cent higher because our cost of living would be 30 per cent lower. The Japanese cars, for example, reflect the policy of the federal government toward manufactured imports. The import duty on manufactured clothing is 40 per cent but we don't get any more than the world market price for our wood, copper, natural gas or hydro-electric power, and we certainly pay more than the world market price for cars, sinks, refrigerators, stoves or television sets — for everything that we need. And they wonder why our cost of living is so high and they wonder why the wage demands of our labor unions are high but it's all a reflection of the fact that everything we need costs more than it does in central Canada. Union demands are a reflection of the cost of living of the average person.''

Easy to argue the point, perhaps, but not so easy to argue some others; and certainly you cannot argue away the anger and hurt and plain confusion that you sense in British Columbia. This, incidentally, seems to be true of most parts of Canada, with the exception of southern Ontario.

But it's the political hopelessness of achieving economic change that radicalizes Christie and probably Marie the panhandler as well. He's just more articulate about it. Panhandling is the only job Marie could find. At that point I think she ceases to be a panhandler; she is self-employed. Society has failed her. At least she hasn't tattooed ''FTW'' on her arm.

Doug Christie is neither a gracious nor imposing man. He has that abrasive and mildly theatrical demeanor common to many small town criminal lawyers. Nor is he particularly controversial or important in himself. At best he can claim 1,500 supporters in a province of more than two and a half million — a mere handful of dissidents who have paid their five dollars to join his Committee for Western Independence. But as he outlines his case, both historically and by listing the various economic and political grievances inflicted by Confederation, by Central Canada, by the Montreal-Toronto power bloc, he becomes disturbingly rational and irritatingly difficult for an easterner to refute. Consider a brief extract from a speech made to the North Vancouver Chamber of Commerce by Gordon Winters, one of the Committee's directors:

Ontario has a population of 8,834,000; Quebec 6,285,000 and British Columbia 2,512,000. Ontario currently has 88 seats in the House of Commons, Quebec 74 and British Columbia 23. But if British Columbia is entitled to only 23 seats then the two large central provinces are over-represented since the population basis would give Ontario 81 seats, not 88; Quebec 58 seats, not 74. That means that Ontario and Quebec have

*between them 23 seats more than they should have. But the
great political robbery doesn't stop there. Newfoundland has
500,000 people and seven seats; Prince Edward Island 122,000
people — not quite as many as Burnaby or Surrey — and they
have four seats. Nova Scotia has 836,000 people and 11 seats
and New Brunswick 694,000 people and ten seats, which means
a combined Maritime population of 2,210,000 people has 33
seats. Remember, British Columbia, with 2,512,000 people has
23 seats.*

I WOULD hear variations of this wherever I went except,
oddly enough, in southern Ontario and Quebec, and now the
federal government has finally implemented redistribution in
time for the next election. Why it took so long is still a question.

As for Quebec, Christie thinks separatism is "noble
madness" (and very useful, too). "Freedom for Quebec," he
told me, "would be a precedent for freedom in western
Canada. Personally I feel that René Lévesque is a moral giant
and that Trudeau is an intellectual giant. I respect morality
more than I do intellectual capacity. In the sense of being ready
to sacrifice economic interests [something no British
Columbian in his right mind would ever consider] for language
and cultural reasons, Lévesque is showing greater dedication,
greater devotion to principle than they [the Québécois] have in
the past . . . . Quebec is prepared to sever the tie with Canada;
that's certainly the intention of Lévesque and his party and, I
think, of a great many more people in Quebec than the Prime
Minister and the media would have us believe."

There's a certain amount of political bafflegab there, and a
certain amount of truth. I share Christie's view of René
Lévesque as a politician of rare integrity and principle but
neither polls nor the people I have talked to have convinced me
that he has, or even thinks he has, a clear mandate to take
Quebec out of Confederation. For one thing he hasn't got the
numbers: true separatists are a minority in Quebec today,
although that could change. A headline in *Maclean's Magazine*
shortly after Lévesque's election summed it up neatly: Lévesque

can only propose separation; English Canada can make it inevitable.

There is unquestionably as much separatist sentiment in the west as there is in Quebec and sometimes I think that while it would take gross political and legal mismanagement in Ottawa and throughout English Canada to lose our most colorful province, it would only take a moment's madness, a series of eastern political blunders, for British Columbia and Alberta to become seriously interested in secession. Whether you agree with them or not, they *know* they could improve their lot that way. It doesn't make much sense to trade with people who are a mountain range and several thousand miles distant when you have an enormous market that begins just a few miles south — not unless you have powerful bonds with the people who live so far to the east. And the most dedicated Péquiste knows he'd pay a terrible price for sovereignty in Quebec.

As for British Columbia, Doug Christie and his Committee for Western Independence are doomed. Christie is far too patient, perhaps too timid; he wants to build his 1,500 supporters into a movement of 50,000 before he makes his move and he simply doesn't have the time. There are more militant, less patient men who have already begun to push him aside.

Chief of these is Ed Fleming, the 39-year-old managing director of an aircraft company and president of the Western Canada Party which split from Christie's committee late in 1976. Fleming claims he has a million dollars worth of pledges and more than 5,000 committed members. "Christie," he said, "is taking the 15-year 'René Lévesque route'," and British Columbia simply won't wait that long. "If we don't get out of Confederation soon, this country will drag British Columbia down the tube. We want action and we want it now." He's planning a leadership convention, won't be a candidate, and says "We'll have all the money we need before the next election."

Premier Bill Bennett isn't worried. He claims that Canada will remain united but under a different form of federalism. Last fall he observed that the Canadian people have worked long and hard "to build a country from sea to sea and we will not allow it to disintegrate at this first challenge [Lévesque, not Fleming] to the future of our country . . . . I believe that we should recognize that the realities of Canada today demand a new type of federalism — regional federalism — one that more properly allows the provinces and regions of our country to develop their own destinies, not separate from Canada but in unity with each other.''

AND THEN there's Bill (Cornflakes) Vander Zalm, not a moderate man but no political lightweight, either. He's Premier Bennett's Human Resources Minister (a neat euphemism for welfare) and he's on record as saying he'd lose no sleep over Quebec's separation because ''among other things it would mean cheaper breakfast cereal without a bilingual label to worry about.'' What he told a *Vancouver Province* reporter the day after Lévesque's victory was:

Certainly I wouldn't lose any sleep if Quebec separates. I doubt, frankly, if there are too many people who would lose very much sleep if they were to separate. I don't think it matters very much. I don't think the people, frankly, are all that concerned about what happens in Quebec. I think it was designed to come about and they'll have their say and they can go whichever way they please. The decision they separate, I don't think it is all that bad. For one thing I'm sure there will be considerable savings to the populace generally, that we won't have to have two printings on every cornflakes box or whatever it might be. So there are things to consider and I don't think we need to worry . . . . I'm one of those anglophones who is considerably frustrated and fed up with the English and the French on everything.

Vander Zalm has also predicted that Canada will self-destruct under the weight of separatist campaigns unless we bring the constitution home and set ourselves up as the United States of Canada. ''The country would be divided into five regions which will have greater jurisdiction over local affairs than provincial governments now have,'' he said. ''We'll still have a federal government but it will be limited to such programs as national defence . . . ." Presumably he'd let Ottawa continue with external affairs, too, although he might balk at immigration.

"People are fed up with the present arrangement," he said. "I'm fed up with what's been happening in the federal government, particularly over this bilingualism hogwash. And unless these problems are resolved, separatist movements will gain strength and we will see the end of Canada." And there you have the best and worst of Bill Vander Zalm, the day after they elected René Lévesque.

And simultaneously you have Ed Fleming saying "our hope is to have enough members [of the Western Canada Party] to put pressure on Victoria to call an election within a year. And if we're successful, British Columbia would secede automatically. . . . We'd be the richest country in the world if we weren't tied to the squandering east. We'd plan for a tax haven and free port to attract investment."

All of which is the political truth, which is to say it sounds convincing and makes good copy. But political truth is often far from factual reality, although there has to be something to it or people would reject it out of hand. That's what makes the separatist fad so dangerous: it's a particularly fertile field for demagoguery and irresponsibility. Certainly there are legitimate grievances which must be resolved. But they go a good deal deeper than bilingual labels on boxes of breakfast cereals, or vague dreams of a Bahamas-like tax haven. Argentina North.

On the other hand the Committee for Western Independence's methodical and devastating analysis of disproportionate parliamentary representation is factual and cannot safely be ignored.

THERE WAS, of course, a Sasquatch sighting while I was in Vancouver, duly reported and duly denied. A 28-year-old bus driver named Pat Lindquist, also a part-time commerce student at the University of British Columbia, a man regarded as sensible and level-headed by his co-workers and not, according to his employers, in the habit of reporting unusual creatures, told a press conference organized by his company, Pacific Stage Lines, that he saw what he thought was a man dressed in a monkey costume. He stopped the bus and went after him and came face to face with a seven-foot-tall, hairy creature which was gazing at him intently with deeply inset eyes. The confrontation at about twenty yards lasted five seconds, at which point Lindquist wisely and rapidly returned to his bus. His passengers didn't believe him but later he returned to the scene with a group of them and some RCMP personnel and they found footprints that measured fifteen by seven inches, with a stride of fifty-five inches, and plaster casts were taken. Much later, after I had returned home, I heard that this "sighting" too had been pronounced a hoax, although the perpetrator was unknown. The Sasquatch is and has for many years been a reliable source of rainy day copy for the British Columbia newspapers, and since they have many rainy days in Lotus Land who would begrudge them their mysterious Sasquatch?

Labor problems and unemployment statistics provide even more rainy day copy and who knows what the real picture is? Within a three-day period last fall I read (in eastern papers, of course) that there has been an unprecedented period of peacefulness within British Columbia's labor unions but that this will end abruptly when wage controls are lifted; that British Columbia has the third highest rate of unemployment west of the Maritimes.

I'm not sure precisely why I mention this, nor what it has to do with Canadian unity, but over the years the British Columbians I have met have struck me as eccentric, oddly defensive and even chauvinistic about their province. Once, in 1971, I travelled with then Leader of the Opposition, Robert Stanfield, on assignment for the *Toronto Telegram* on a coast to coast tour. We reached Vancouver at the height of the worst blizzard they'd had for several decades and the snow was at least two feet deep. I called a friend — a close friend whom I'd known well when he and his wife lived for a while in Toronto and whom I hadn't seen in several years — and he was angry, furious in fact, that I had finally visited his homeland at its absolute climatic worst. Listen, I'm not joking: his anger permanently damaged our friendship. And when I told Stanfield this he said he'd had similar experiences and had learned never, in political speeches, to make jokes about the weather.

Then there was a night in Toronto when a group of ex-Vancouverites — these friends of mine included — threw a party. Arrangements had been made with an Air Canada pilot somebody knew to bring us a large, fresh-caught salmon which we would devour with due respect. It was a disaster. All the Vancouver people, men and women alike, went into the kitchen to confer on the proper method of steaming a salmon; each had a minutely different system and it turned into a donnybrook which wrecked the party. The salmon, of course, was delicious.

British Columbians *are* different, a casually friendly denim society, generous and warm but prone to moodiness, strange cults and offbeat politics. The thought of losing them, either to the vagaries of mini-nationhood or to the evils of statehood, sickens me. And of course it has to be one of the most spectacularly beautiful parts of Canada. I had to fly to Victoria to make my appointment with Doug Christie but I took the ferry back. The sun was setting, the evening mists made magic of the mountains and I claim them as my own, the people too: part of my birthright as a Canadian.

But will I need a passport someday to visit the Pacific Coast? I'm damned if I'll ever accept such a prospect, not without a bloody good fight, and I feel the same way about Quebec. But armed intervention? That would be intolerable. I have friends on the coast. I have family in Quebec. There has to be a constitutional compromise that will make this country work, and we'd better find it damn quick. When the slush clogs the streets of Toronto each winter and I'm sardined in the subway I think of the softer climate, the warmth of the people on the west coast, and I think of their sense of isolation from the east and I begin to believe we've transcended eccentricity: we're mad as hatters, every one of us.

A FEW WEEKS later I would meet an old friend on a bus somewhere in New Brunswick and he would tell me that Quebec is what makes Canada interesting, and that he wouldn't want anything to do with a Canada that did not include Quebec. He'd as soon be American, he said. He spoke with some emotion which sets him apart from Charles Connaghan, who seems a cool, corporate executive and the last person you'd expect to find single-handedly organizing a powerful movement apparently intent on pushing water uphill. Nor does Connaghan appear to have any deep affection for the people of Quebec, although I could be very wrong about that. He's a tough-minded Irishman who doesn't wear his heart on his sleeve. He understands that western isolation has more to do with distance than race; British Columbians feel isolated from the rest of Canada *including* Quebec. It's more a problem of apathy and ignorance than dislike or mistrust, and he has dedicated himself to persuading British Columbians not only that they need Quebec but that they must persuade the people of Quebec that they feel this way.

Chuck Connaghan is the 45-year-old administrative vice-president of the University of British Columbia. Before that he was a formidable labor negotiator for the British Columbian construction industry. They used to call him "Mr. Lockout" in those days. He doesn't like the "redneck" image and he didn't like the "let 'em go" reaction to the Lévesque election. "It was unfortunate," he told me. "I went to a dinner party one night and I was getting beaten around the ears because I said we just couldn't afford to let them go."

"I don't think we really understand what the problem with Confederation is. For one thing we have the isolation of the west coast, there's no doubt about it. I spent nine years of my life in Ontario and Quebec and I've been back here about seven years and there is an isolationist mentality that develops."

Since the French segment of British Columbia's population is relatively small, any perceived francophone or bilingualist threat must come from Ottawa and not from Coquitlam (excluding those dratted cereal packages and the *mode d'emploi* on everything else).

I asked him why we couldn't, as he put it, "afford" to let Quebec go and he said "because within a generation you'd see the west go. British Columbia and Alberta. As one man, an Albertan, told me 'we're prepared to pay the tariffs and the protections to keep Quebec in Confederation but I don't think we'd be prepared to pay that for southern Ontario.' I don't know how widespread that is but I think it could become central to the problem, and that's where the danger lies, in not doing anything at all. We're prepared to pay the price to keep Quebec but if Quebec goes, that's the end of the pay-off, the tariff wall. The particular thing that sticks in the craw is the freight rates, of course. We see a net output of dollars from this province. Some think it's going to Quebec; *I* think it's going to the Maritimes."

The usual buzz word is "equalization payments" and it refers to that portion of personal income tax and other taxes that goes to Ottawa, where it is channeled into welfare cheques, industrial development schemes, farm or coal mine subsidies and other federally supported programs. The wealthy provinces pay large sums of money which eventually go to the have-not provinces. There's a certain justification for this, particularly to socialist-minded people. The purpose is to share the national wealth, to shore up sagging provincial economies, and to maintain the illusion of national or nation-wide affluence.

Quebec has traditionally been regarded as a have-not province, although there has been much debate over this point recently. What Connaghan is saying, and I think that many agree with him, is that he doesn't mind supporting Quebec through such equalization payments, despite the fact that they drain British Columbia's economy, but that if Quebec were to secede he, or his Albertan friend, would be damned if Ontario should become a beneficiary. He doesn't care whether the money goes to Quebec or the Maritimes, as long as it isn't going to Ontario.

There are some ironic resonances with what separatists like

Doug Christie and Ed Fleming (and still others in Alberta, northern Ontario and New Brunswick) are saying despite the fact that Connaghan and Christie are on opposite sides of the fence. Both agree that British Columbia is being ripped off by Confederation, whether in terms of freight rates or tariffs, or arbitrary limits imposed by Ottawa on what they can charge for their raw materials and resources. Neither man, for example, will argue that Confederation is working. Both are suspicious if not openly hostile to Central Canada at least in abstract terms [it isn't *us* they hate so much as what they think we're doing to them]. Doug Christie, Ed Fleming and Bill Vander Zalm don't really care what Quebec does, they simply want British Columbia to be free, perhaps within a revised constitution but more likely, according to Christie and Fleming, outside. Connaghan, on the other hand, wants to persuade Quebeckers that Canada needs them and appreciates them even if we can't always speak to them in their own language.

Connaghan's quest began in an Ottawa hotel elevator last year, the morning after René Lévesque's speech to members of the financial community in New York City. "I heard two ladies saying in French what a wonderful, first-class speech Lévesque had made. And then in the corridor I heard two Anglophones muttering about what a terrible speech it was. On the plane back to Vancouver I read both French and English newspaper accounts and it was as though they were reporting two different speeches."

English reporters zapped Lévesque, stressing the cool reception he got. French writers did the opposite, stressing the positive aspects of the speech not seeming to notice that the applause was less than overwhelming. It's a common enough phenomenon in journalism, but only evident to bilingual readers like Connaghan who bother to compare such reports.

When he returned to Vancouver Chuck Connaghan began telephoning friends (and former associates and even enemies) to find out if they, too, were concerned by what they were hearing. They were, and Connaghan proposed a meeting to discuss what they thought the issues were, and whether they thought there was anything useful that individuals or small groups of them could do about it.

"We got about twenty-five people together," he said, "and I got the feeling that if I'd had time I could have got 1,500. We agreed to meet regularly and that we would not name our association: it might be regarded as a political party. We are interested in raising awareness in British Columbia of Quebec, and also in Quebec of what British Columbians think. We are all of the mind that Canada without Quebec is as unthinkable as Canada without British Columbia."

Connaghan believes that the Quebec referendum, when it comes, will not be decided on the basis of politics, economics or legalities but purely on emotion. "There must," he says, "be absolutely no confusion or mistake in the minds of the people of Quebec that we want them to stay in Canada and that we want them to be part of a strong Canada.

"If that means we have to look at federalism in a different light, that some things are going to have to change, then fine — the stakes are far too great for us not to do that. I'm not taking Christie seriously, I'm more concerned with the domino theory. I have a great deal of faith that we can keep Canada together. It's a matter of finding an acceptable formula that will make it stronger."

That may prove difficult and Connaghan admits it. "Whatever Quebec gets, every other province is going to have to have too," he told me. "There's a danger in not doing anything at all and letting Quebec go by default. But if a deal is made with Quebec that isn't given to the other provinces then we'll have a larger problem than we do today with Quebec." On the other hand, Connaghan admitted that "that's a pretty forceful argument the Prime Minister put forth in Winnipeg. He said there are five million people who speak French. That's as many people as there are on the prairies. It gets home to you that you're not just dealing with another province. We're two and a half million people in this province and yet it's the third largest province in the country . . ."

It's confusing to be reasonable. Perhaps that's why so few of us are.

Nor is Connaghan alone. There are at least four other groups in British Columbia committed to persuading the people of Quebec that if they aren't always loved out west, neither are they universally despised; certainly they are wanted and needed as Canadians. Worthwhile marriages have been salvaged by such novel approaches before. Companionship and mutual need become at least as important as love, and both Westerners and Quebeckers are most companionable people. Mind you, they don't know each other very well. There are many British Columbians who have never met anyone east of Alberta and the opposite is equally true. Furthermore, until very recently the Vancouver newspapers printed very little about French Canadian aspirations and exasperations. Three thousand miles, even in this electronic age, is a formidable barrier to understanding.

"I'm talking about a populist movement," Connaghan told a Toronto newspaper reporter, "in which the average British Columbian says to the average Quebecker: 'Look, forget the politicians. I'm telling you that as a Canadian who lives in British Columbia I want you as a part of Canada. You're a Canadian living in Quebec. I recognize you've got a cultural heritage, a language heritage. I want you to know that as a West Coaster I have a certain kind of heritage too — maybe not as clearly defined as yours, but it is there. It is this diversity that can give our country great strength.

'If you need protection for your heritage, then you will have my backing . . . . and I want your help to protect my kind of heritage.' "

Connaghan plans a very quiet revolution. First a series of meetings, later a speakers' bureau. "We want to raise the awareness of British Columbians to the problem and to transmit the message to Quebec that we care. We'd invite people like Abbé Dionne of Laval, some French Canadian business people, labor people. We can't move fast, we're a long way from Quebec and a lot of our people have never been to Quebec."

He asked me for my perception of British Columbia's role — for my opinion of his scheme, I suppose — and I told him, somewhat brutally perhaps, that in terms of Quebec and the referendum, British Columbia seemed "pretty irrelevant. They — the people of Quebec — seem to have made up their minds.

Separation, economic union, I don't know what." I've had to revise my opinion since then but at the time the quiet resolve of his response disturbed me, perhaps moved me a little. He looked thoughtfully out the window for a moment and began talking, almost to himself. "That's interesting, what you say about the irrelevancy of the provinces, and I suspect you're right, but we see it a different way, some of us. Maybe it's the arrogance of British Columbia again, but we think we can play a role, Alberta and British Columbia . . ."

He expressed concern about apathy, about the uncommitted and said "Suppose the people of Canada are faced in the near future with having to vote on a referendum for a deal for Quebec. I think we've got to be prepared for that and I don't think people can vote intelligently unless they've had some communication about what's going on in Quebec, what the problem is."

"Has it ever occurred to you," I asked, "that Canada, as a nation, is preposterous?"

"Oh sure," he said. "That's what fascinates me. If you and I were to sit down and put something like Canada on paper, and start from scratch, we'd probably end up by saying it would never work. Unmanageable. It'll never fly. We keep asking 'What's a Canadian?'"

"What," I asked, "is a Canadian?"

"I really . . . I don't think there's an answer."

"Then what is it you're trying to save?"

"I'm saving a country that is different from the United States," he said, "different from the United Kingdom, different from Europe. It has attractions in terms of environment. We have a different mentality from the United States. One of the things that makes us different is Quebec."

We parted on that note. I was feeling somewhat subdued. I often feel that way when I'm in the presence of people I admire, but whose quests seem improbable. I wish him well but I keep wondering: does he have the time?

I HAD DINNER that night with an old friend, a journalist, and his family. Barbecued salmon and idle chat about my own improbable quest, about Canada and what it means to Canadians. He listened to my adventures and agreed that there are a lot of groups in the province, drawing on a lot of dissatisfactions and grievances for their support. "It's not exactly Confederation, either," he said, "but the continuing way the government in Ottawa has been running this country."

"Not Confederation?"

"No," he said, "I figure Canadian politics isn't working. I'm no fan of the Liberals. Unemployment is big, you're right about that, and inflation is really a problem. The number one market for our lumber is the United States but we're in direct competition with the state of Washington. We're more dependent on the northern states and the Pacific Rim countries. The Japanese, for example, are getting more and more into our system of housing construction [meaning increased plywood sales]. Did you know that there are people here, in mining and lumber, who have bilingual business cards? English on one side, Japanese on the other."

"No," I said, "I didn't."

Hıs WIFE was more concerned with sports, and she was bitter. "We pay through the teeth to see professional sports. It doesn't matter to me whether we win or not, we could lose year after year and it would be OK. But we pay all these prices and we get all these so-called great professionals in and they bomb, they really bomb. Then they move to Philadelphia, like Bob Daly who's responsible for Philadelphia's goals, or football players who move to the Hamilton Tiger Cats or the Toronto Argos and they perform magnificently and this has been going on for years and nobody's ever figured it out."

"It's too soft a climate," her husband put in. "They get out here and they relax. They take it easy."

I REMEMBER a couple of years ago, visiting a couple of doctors who lived on an island about a hundred miles north of

Vancouver. There had been a fantastic flight up the Georgia Strait, the magnificent Rockies on my right, Vancouver Island and then the Pacific Ocean on my left, the sun shining overhead: a glorious day. When I walked into the doctors' living room and looked out their picture window I couldn't help myself. I burst out laughing, guffawing, almost, the tears streaming from my eyes. They began to look offended so I controlled myself and tried to explain. When I am home and look out my study window I see my backyard, pleasant enough but not one of Toronto's spectacular beauty spots. When I look out the front windows I see a pleasant enough street lined with modest homes, high rise apartment buildings looming behind them. My summers are hot and my winters cold and wet, with slush-clogged streets.

That picture window was a parody of itself, pure Norman Rockwell perfection. Mountains on either side, neatly framing the picturesque fishing village below, the quaint little fishing boats moored in the fjord. Just then their telephone rang and a neighbor was asking if they could use a salmon or two; he'd caught more than he needed that morning. Paradise. I tried to explain the irony of it all, this final culmination of West Coast beauty contrasted with the dull discomforts of life in Central Canada but I don't think I succeeded. It was pure envy on my part and it struck me as enormously funny. But yes, the climate is soft and the living looks easy.

FURTHER NORTH, on the Queen Charlotte Islands and on the northern mainland, the living is not so easy and federal transport minister Otto Lang has, doubtless for reasons he considers adequate, made it even less so. He achieved this by cutting off a $4.5 million subsidy which had been financing the three 300-foot ferries servicing the upper mainland communities and the Queen Charlotte Islands.

Now four and a half million dollars sounds like a lot of money, and the recipient of this subsidy, Northern Navigation Limited, was serving a total of 18 communities, representing somewhere between twenty and thirty thousand people, of whom approximately six thousand live on the Queen Charlotte Islands. Since the subsidy was cut off two of the ships have been tied up at a Vancouver wharf and the third was sold in California.

Last April an emergency convoy of trucks had to haul food and supplies the 188 miles north to Prince Rupert, on the coast, and Terrace, fifty or sixty miles inland. The towns involved paid for the convoy and prices have risen by as much as 85 per cent. And Delta, B.C., MLA Walter Davidson growled that the B.C. ferry system "is the only one in Canada without a federal subsidy. Ottawa," he said, "doesn't believe anything exists west of the Rockies. I hope they recognize us before it's too late."

I was needling someone — I forget who it was — about the size of British Columbia, and the resources, and the fact that there aren't many people living there and most of the ones who do, live within commuting distance of Greater Vancouver (about a million and a half) or in Victoria (about 250,000) and he observed with devastating understatement that, yes, it is a pretty big province but that there are one or two mountains to contend with. They don't show up very clearly on political maps but if you look at a topographical map they show very clearly: rather like Tibet, for the most part.

So I asked my informant why Canada needed those 30,000 rather expensive residents in northern British Columbia. What were they doing for us? Well, he said, "they're mining copper, logging and generally helping to make Canada rich. British Columbia has 80 per cent of Canada's softwood forest wealth and a single coal deposit near Hudson Hope represents twenty per cent of the world's reserves. There's gold, silver, zinc, lead, nickel, copper, asbestos, molybdenum, tungsten, sulphur, iron ore, oil and gas deposits, not to mention water power, perhaps one of the most valuable export commodities of the future. Everything except people, in fact."

Northland Navigation's boats were twenty years old and three years ago the company put in a proposal to Ottawa to upgrade their service. They wanted to build two or three modern ships with roll-on, roll-off cargo handling facilities.

The company was willing to spend $20 million if the government would guarantee a system of declining subsidies which would diminish, after seven years, to about a quarter of a million dollars. The company got no response from Ottawa; the subsidy was cut off and my informant said, in genuine anguish, "These people are suffering. Otto Lang is from Saskatchewan. If anybody in Canada should understand transportation, and how, historically, to get it has required subsidies, *he* should. Those damned prairies and their railway lines. This shipping service up and down the coast is a water railway."

Never mind, the federal government is now paying a whopping $7,500,000 subsidy to the BC Ferries Corporation which will doubtless get around to providing adequate service to the north and to the Queen Charlotte Islands someday. "But," said my informant, "people think of British Columbia as bitchy and regionalist, with nothing to bitch about and here you have a situation where people are suffering because of a bureaucratic decision in far away Ottawa, made by people who either don't understand or don't care what happens to these communities. And the people up on the coast had to truck in twenty tons of food."

Well there's bitchiness and there's bitchiness. I'd only been in British Columbia a few days and it seemed to me they had much to bitch about. Recently the *Vancouver Province* published a brief and poignant editorial which a friend gave to me. It was titled "Communications Canada" and the text follows:

You don't need a degree in the social sciences to realize that a large part of B.C.'s resentment, envy or suspicion of Central Canada is caused by the remoteness of the West Coast.

Even Pierre Trudeau and his Liberal friends cannot erase the thousands of miles. But he and they can do something to see that modern technology is used to limit the effects of distance on both actions and attitudes.

Yet, although Air Canada and CP Air planes take only a few hours to fly from Toronto, mail from Central Canada takes up to a week. During the Christmas-New Year holiday, mail from the east and Europe was taking up to a month.

Government departments in B.C. hear about the govern-ment's decisions from the media. Parliamentary bills, reports and other documents take a week or more to reach B.C. Yet there are frequent flights from the East, often with space in their freight holds.

Newspapers from other provinces are rarely seen in Vancouver newsstands. They are usually too old and too ex-pensive to attract the interested reader. Yet during these times, rapid distribution of reasonably priced newspapers from Montreal and Halifax and other cities would help Canadians here understand the problems of the East. And who knows, the advent of B.C. papers in Ottawa, Montreal and Toronto might remind Canadians there of the West Coast.

The millions of dollars and the technological inventiveness provided to the CBC so that it can be the great unifier don't seem to have been well spent. How about giving us mail, papers, and information from the East in 20th century times? Perhaps that will succeed.

T HAT DIDN'T sound bitchy to me. It didn't sound wholly accurate, either, but it has the ring of common sense. By now, however, *I* was feeling bitchy, confused and eager to be on my way. I went down to the bus terminal and purchased, for $166, a ticket which would eventually take me to North Sydney, on Cape Breton Island, and from there I'd take a ferry to Port aux Basques, Newfoundland, cross that desolate but friendly island by CN bus (they've taken the trains away from Newfoundland) and ultimately I would reach St. John's. It would take me about a month, but I was on my way, headed for Kamloops, a city of 60,000 people some 264 miles east and I was about to learn my first lesson about Canadian bus travel: it would take me seven and a half hours to get there. I left on Sunday, May 21, at 12:15 p.m., taking a front seat (to avoid the tinted side windows) and for the first time in my life I wasn't sorry to leave Vancouver. I was on my way.

My SEATMATE was a 37-year-old Master Corporal who had been with the Canadian Armed Services for the past twenty years. He was headed for Revelstoke; his father had died in an automobile accident the day before, he had taken compassionate leave and his misfortune was my gain. He distracted himself by talking to me and he had a great deal to say.

He'd served two years at Chibougama, Quebec, and had been put through the four-week French language immersion course, but whenever he tried to use the language shopkeepers would ignore him. That didn't bother him nearly as much as his children being beaten up at school, particularly the time his four-year-old was chased by a hatchet-wielding classmate. All of which might be expected to make a soldier from Revelstoke bitter, and it did. He feels strong resentment toward the French for the treatment he and his family received in Chibougama during those two years, *but he isn't anti-French*. He's pro-French, even pro-Quebec, to some extent.

"I feel the problem is that Trudeau tried to start at the top and he should have started at the bottom," he told me. "Teaching Canadians to speak French would be good for them; knowing a second language expands the mind. It might take two or three generations to make it a truly bilingual country but it would be worth it in the end."

But not with four-week French language immersion courses. No, you start in the schools and let it spread from there as happened with his daughter, who started in kindergarten in Chibougama and speaks the language fluently. Ironically she was the one member of the family who became permanently embittered against Quebec. She simply couldn't forget the hazing she got as a very young child, simply because she was *anglais*.

The corporal is a native of Revelstoke and joined the army at 17. He agrees that the West is being ripped off by the East but he isn't rabid about it — "resigned" was the word he used. There was a depth to the man that eluded me until he mentioned what his job in the army entailed. He deals with nuclear radiation accidents — accidents or leakages involving trucks loaded with hot supplies for hospitals or industries. Not the stereotyped sinecure of the peacetime soldier.

We were quiet for a while, driving north on Highway 1 beside the Fraser River, and he pointed out landmarks, fishladders and the like. Coming into the semi-arid zone just west of the Rockies I was astonished: this is sagebrush country and I hadn't known we had such land. Almost desert. But the corporal told me it was far from that. "If you can grow sagebrush you can grow anything," he said. "All you have to do is add water. I'll show you something in a few minutes."

I watched the countryside rolling by, with lush green fields of hay and wheat here and there. Farmers rig enormous irrigation systems consisting of a fat hose supported by what look like oversized bicycle wheels. The hose is flexible and a man simply pushes it along, a few yards at a time, until the whole length has been advanced and the width of the field is sprayed that way. Ingenious and effective: wherever the system ended the desert resumed. It reminded me of the circular farms of Israel.

Then the corporal tapped me on the knee and pointed half way up a hill, to some long-forgotten wooden remains which snaked along beside us. Some time before World War Two a group of homesteaders settled here, he said. Not very many, just a few families. There was plenty of water in the Fraser River but no way to raise it to the fields so they built themselves a wooden aqueduct in the style of the ancient Romans, bringing water from an elevated lake some six or seven miles distant. "When the war came the men joined up and the aqueduct gradually fell apart — it took a lot of maintaining — and the families drifted away to other parts. But for a while there were lush crops growing there, tobacco leaves as tall as a man."

I watched for traces of those rotting timbers and thought of the enormous effort it must have taken, the confidence; I reflected on the Master Corporal who dealt with radioactive mishaps, traveling stoically to his father's funeral and describing to me with pride and enthusiasm the land he knew and loved. I began to feel cleansed of the tensions of separatism and alienation, and found myself exulting in both the sheer grandeur of the scenery and the sheer guts of men long gone and he must have sensed my mood; we didn't do much talking after that. Perhaps he was thinking of his father. I was thinking of my country, the audacity of creating it and the lunacy of letting it fall apart like that magnificent aqueduct. Not to mention the man sitting next to me, whose children had been beaten up because they were *anglais* and whose response, tinged with bitterness, was that all Canadian children should be taught to be bilingual not just to save a country but because it would expand their minds.

The bus rolled into Kamloops more or less on schedule and I booked a room at the Plaza Hotel, somewhat surprised to find a man ahead of me in the lobby, with backpack slung over one shoulder, propping up a 10-speed bicycle as he signed the register. My mind wasn't functioning very clearly — it had been a long ride on the bus — and I watched him check in and wheel his bike into the elevator. I checked in, showered and came down to the bar — a glass of cold beer is a wonderful antidote to seven and a half hours on even the most comfortable of buses. I had to step over a couple of men who were wrestling on the floor, whether in anger or play I couldn't tell until later, when a giggling woman joined them.

Halfway through my second beer the penny dropped: what in the hell was a grown man doing in the lobby of a hotel in the middle of nowhere with a 10-speed bike? I dashed into the lobby and asked the receptionist for his name and room number and went up and knocked on the door. "Who is it?" he asked.

"Are you Paul Clark?" I said. "I'm a writer and I'd like to talk to you." He opened the door, somewhat surprised, pleaded for shower time, and agreed to meet me downstairs in half an hour. "Great," I said, "I'll be there."

Paul Clark, 21 years old, is from Windsor, Ontario but had spent the past eight months squatting on the Queen Charlotte Islands, eating clams, fasting one day each week, reflecting on the world that confronts him. He was riding home to Windsor, that's all. He'd already eaten so he talked while I ate. He seemed hard to pigeonhole: I guess he found his Walden Pond on the Queen Charlotte Islands. "Technology's fucked," he told me. "The Indians used to live off fish and clams and thirty per cent of their babies died. Now, with technology, everybody lives, but what kind of a life?" He'd been pondering such things and had decided to spend a while as a recluse to see if he could come up with answers. He'd told his friends what he intended to do, and he was a bit contemptuous of their response. "Friends would say they want to do what I've done but they don't really *know* what I've done. They'd like to do it [break out and think for awhile] but they're not ready yet. But you'll never be ready, you can't wait until you're ready."

It was a matter-of-fact statement. As for Quebec he felt that "separation is greed. They're not happy with the rest of Canada but in the long run they'll only make things worse for us. They're looking at things in a material way, not a universal way."

Paul was very tired and wanted to go to bed; he had a long ride ahead, so that pretty well sums up our conversation. Make of it what you will, and see if you can come up with a category for a man who will spend eight months of his life eating clams (and fasting) on a remote, offshore island and then ride three thousand miles home to visit his folks. I couldn't.

To hell with it. I went to bed. I was looking for some meaning for Canada: he was looking for the meaning of life. Much later, after I'd returned home, I saw a woman on a Toronto street. She was carrying a burlap handbag with her credo printed on it: "I have abandoned my search for truth and am now looking for a good fantasy." I think I'm with her.

SUNDAY MORNING, as I've already recounted, I listened to Flying Phil Gaglardi's sermon on women's liberation, in his Calvary Church, and then I went for a walk. I wound up on a park bench overlooking the river, a replica of one of the old stockaded whiskey forts (closed) behind me and a man about my own age beside me. I was waiting for the bus that would take me to Revelstoke, 131 miles east; he was a railway engineer waiting to go on duty and he told me about the coal trains that go from the open pit mines at Fort Steele up through the Rogers Pass and ultimately to the port of Vancouver.

"They carry 14,500 tons of coal," he said, "and it takes four 1,500 horsepower engines up front, three slave units in the middle and five pushers at the back. That's 18,000 horsepower to push 110 coal cars through the mountains and get this, it takes *ten* of those trains to fill a Japanese freighter."

R<small>EVELSTOKE</small> W<small>AS</small> beautiful but, because of the bus schedule, unproductive, other than giving me a chance to see the Columbia River, the subject of much controversy with the United States for so many years. The Americans badly covet the tons of water that flow along its 1,200-mile length. I arrived in late afternoon and left at 9:50 a.m. the following morning, bound for Calgary, a distance of 258 miles and a seven and a half hour run, which is about as long as I like to stay on a bus (although my record is something over twenty hours, an experience that took me three days to recover from).

T<small>HERE</small> W<small>AS</small> a woman sitting next to me who was infuriating: she was reading a book, ignoring the magnificent panorama of the Rockies. Of course it turned out that she makes the trip so often that she knows the mountains better than I know my own backyard, and when she realized it was new to me she put her book aside and gave me a first rate commentary for about an hour, and then we fell asleep, just beyond Banff.

Just before I began to doze I spotted a crudely painted sign nailed to a tree, with the intriguing comment: "Lumbermen are misfits". I didn't even try to figure that one out.

THE PRAIRIES
Life, Dust and
Alienation

GOD IS important on the prairies. I have that on the authority of Federal Agriculture Minister Eugene Whelan, quoted in a Canadian Press clipping I'd found in the Toronto *Globe and Mail,* when the conception for my Canadian odyssey was germinating. There had been little snow that winter and little rain in the spring and it was beginning to look like a drought.

Whelan did the only sensible thing an agriculture minister could do under the circumstances: he urged his fellow Members of Parliament on both sides of the House to "pray for rain."

"If He's on our side — you know, the one we pray to — He can do us a lot of good," Whelan said in a speech to the House of Commons. The Government, meanwhile, was doing everything it could to prepare for what looked like the worst drought since the dusty depression of the 1930s. That was March 10th. A month later another Canadian Press clipping described an acute labor shortage because hundreds of men were fighting grass fires, and city councillors in Brandon, Manitoba, were debating a water rationing bylaw.

On Tuesday, May 24, we stopped for a lunch break at

Banff and by mid-afternoon the Rockies were behind; the land was flat and passengers were talking about how much rain there had been and wondering whether the wheat that had been planted would take root or simply rot. There had been serious flooding in some towns. No one was talking about drought anymore, but they continued to worry about the wheat. A few days later I would spend an afternoon with a farmer who would give me a chilling education in the economics and vagaries of wheat farming which I would find truly alarming. God is indeed important on the prairies. And so is Alberta's Premier, Peter Lougheed, a man desperately aware of the uncertainties of a wheat-based economy and frustrated in his attempts to use his province's vast oil revenues to diversify and strengthen the economy. His situation is almost biblical. Excluding the potential of the tar sands (and the Americans got the better end of that deal) and the heavy oil, Alberta has about thirty years of conventional crude oil revenues remaining. Like Joseph, he wants to use the thirty fat years to see the province through the lean years that may follow. Prairie farmers have endured lean years and fear them as few Canadians can fully comprehend.

Lougheed empathizes, as do many Westerners, with Quebec. "This country is without doubt a richer, greater, united country with Quebec a full partner and this province [Alberta] and our citizens will work together to maintain a united Canada," he told a Progressive Conservative conference in Edmonton. But he warned that "there must be a shift of decision-making westward from Toronto . . . there must be a reduction to a marked degree, of the interference and obstacles to our objectives by the Federal Government."

It was a message that would be hammered at me for the next eleven days; indeed, it became an overwhelmingly dominant theme through my entire journey. It always seemed facile, to me, for provincial governments to blame all their problems on Ottawa. It no longer does, at least not to the same extent.

I SPENT THE first night in Calgary at the Sheraton Summit

Hotel and I fully intended to spend a quiet evening in my room, dutifully writing up my notes and planning a useful itinerary for the next few days. First, a quiet moment in the Library Lounge (the books are real but their covers are glued together so you can't pull out a single volume; you'd have to bring out a whole shelf-full) and some desultory conversation with an American computer programmer. He both bothered and intrigued me, and I wondered if he was aware of what's happening in Canada or whether he even cared. He didn't, and eventually I gave up on him. He'd never been to Canada before and had no interest in the country and finally, perhaps as a hint that I should leave him alone, he opened his briefcase. There, in that briefcase, were perhaps thirty or forty felt-tipped pens every color in the rainbow, lined up like troops for his inspection. I asked him if I could look at his coloring book and he huffily explained that the many-colored pens were essential to his business. His coloring books were yards of computer print-outs which required elaborate and colorful decoration to make them comprehensible to his clients. I left in disgust, to find myself a hamburger and take a brief walk along the 8th Street Mall. "Teenagers' wasteland," they call it, which I think unfair. Probably as unfair as calling Calgary "Dallas North".

I saw a group of teenagers watching a city street cleaner pushing along a two-can dolly and sweeping up the garbage from the street. One of the youths asked him if he could have his job and he just smiled and continued his work. I talked with them for a while and found them clean, pleasant, and busily screwing up Canada's labor statistics. They were definitely looking for work and not finding any, so they become part of the great Canadian army of unemployed. But it's *work* they're looking for, not *jobs*, a difference both considerable and damaging.

"See, what I want," a red-headed youth told me, "is about two or three weeks of 14-hour days. There's a big bash coming up in New Mexico and I want to go, but I've only got $200 and I need at least another $200." Another youth said he'd been promised a job as a security guard but that he needed $50 for ID and bonding and he didn't have it, and the others were twitting him about the job he had that he didn't have. I tried to steer the conversation toward broader matters and they reacted by intensifying their jocularity and tinging it with disdain, whether for me or their own alienation I don't know. Probably both. Certainly they weren't losers. Hell, they weren't even participants; they wanted to work long enough to achieve their ends, whether a "big bash in New Mexico" or merely to establish their right to claim unemployment insurance and we raised them that way, back in the late 1950s and early 1960s and I don't know how. I've talked with parents of such people and found them confused, hard-working, intelligent and disappointed in their offspring.

Later I met a man from Toronto. His name was Ken and he owned a couple of racehorses and was in Calgary for a meet. He wanted to talk and dragged me to the Four Brothers Restaurant, an establishment where he was well known and warmly greeted. He bought me a huge steak dinner and I learned more about the horse racing business than I wanted to know. He was in his early sixties, I think; his wife was dead and all he had left was a daughter he adored, his horses and, apparently, a great deal of money.

A hooker came in and spotted right away where the money was. She slithered up to Ken asking if he wanted "a good time"; he looked at her somewhat lugubriously and said, "All I got in my pockets is $19, sweetheart."

"What about you?" she said, turning toward me with insulting pessimism on her painted face.

"Do you take Chargex?" I asked, as innocently as I could, and she flounced off, leaving us in hysterics. Eventually the restaurant closed and I tottered off to bed. My only real regret was that Ken's *only* interests were his daughter and his horses. He had absolutely no opinions on Quebec, national unity, western alienation or anything remotely useful. Well, he did give me a hot tip on the Queen's Plate but I forgot to write it down.

Next day I slept late, worked long, dined out with friends and it was about 11:30 p.m. when I got back to my hotel and heard music coming from the lounge. Another half hour wasn't going to kill me, and that's how I met the Canadian Texan. Canadian by citizenship, Texan by birth and by nature. He was 47 years old, wearing a white suit and a white cowboy hat with silver medallions on the hatband, grumbling at the folksinger who either didn't know or wouldn't sing "The Streets of Laredo". He came in, he told me, "to drink myself to the point where I can just get myself home to bed." He dreaded the moment he woke each morning, realizing he had to face yet another day. He works as a seismic crew cook in the winters and goes "into the bush" when he can in the summer. He was very annoyed once, he told me, when a Chinese bartender told him to take off his hat.

"Hell," he said, "it's a tradition in this town — or was — that if you ever made your living as a cowboy you wear your hat in a bar. And now I can't even go back to that place," he added dolefully. "That Chinese owned it."

He pointed to his glass of beer and told me that's what killed his wife, fifteen years ago. She was a Blackfoot Indian and the only love he ever had and she died of alcoholism at the age of 35. Maybe it was loneliness. "I was away a lot so either she's unfaithful to me or she drinks. She was faithful so she drank and Indians can't drink. She started on beer, then whiskey, then wine and then death."

His face and neck were heavily scarred, from Korea and Vietnam, he said. He'd been with the 82nd Airborne and he hates gooks and longs for death and doesn't care a hoot about Quebec. "If Quebec goes the Stars and Stripes will fly over the West," he said. "Hell, that's where all the money comes from anyway."

Redneck? I don't know. I saw him as a lonely, embittered man who, at 47, has absolutely nothing to look forward to. He'd won a few medals but a woman hocked them for $30. He figures pretty soon we'll join forces with the Russians to fight the Chinese. "Has to be," he said. He hates gooks and he married a Blackfoot and when she died he stopped living. I went to bed very depressed that night. I'd met a series of wasted, lonely men and turned-off teenagers living in one of the most fortunate countries in the world, a nation crying for involvement, and all I was finding was apathy, self-pity, alienation and despair. Absolute insanity. And tragic waste.

WEDNESDAY WAS the day I had an appointment with A. M. Harradence, QC, at two o'clock sharp. Sharp for me, anyway; he was half an hour late and bustled me into his lavish office on the eighth floor of one of Calgary's slicker office buildings. In fact it's the slickest office building I've ever been in that has only cold water in the lavatory. The eighth-floor lavatory, anyway.

Never mind. Milt Harradence greeted me warmly, the firm western bone-crushing handshake, the broad, confident smile. Harradence is the unofficial but inevitable spokesman for the Western National Association, which is dedicated to the establishment of Alberta as a sovereign nation within less than two years. Doug Christie, the separatist lawyer in Victoria, had told me about him and I'd asked him to call Harradence to tell him I'd be coming, hoping for an interview. The two men represent separate provincial organizations but with more or less identical goals: freedom from the economic shackles of the East. Canada's crawling with separatists, it seems, and there may well be more of them outside Quebec than in.

I was overwhelmed by the warmth of Milt Harradence's greeting until he said, still smiling broadly, that he'd like to see some ID. I was stunned, almost speechless as I reached for my wallet. "What would you like?" I asked. "Driver's licence? Credit cards? I haven't got my birth certificate with me, I had to send it to Ottawa for a new passport and I haven't carried a press card for years. Anyway, I thought Doug Christie had called you about me."

"He did, Mr. Aitken, but let's face it. I don't know you from Adam." He browsed, still smiling warmly, through the pieces of plastic and paper that establish me as a guaranteed and appropriately identified human being, and returned them to me saying "I also called Walter Stewart [then managing editor] at *Maclean's Magazine* to check on you."

"My God," I said, "I haven't worked there for three years at least."

"Well, he gave you a glowing recommendation," he said [thank you, Walter]. Now, I thought, the interview might proceed, but no, Mr. Harradence wanted me to know that he was armed. He pulled a vicious little handgun from his pocket and told me it was a Walther PPK [James Bond's favorite weapon, remember?], removed the clip and took the bullets out of it, and also the one in the barrel. I'd already turned on my tape recorder and the clicking sounds of that gun made me shiver when I was doing the transcript later.

"Why," I asked, "do you carry a gun?"

"The permit," he answered, "says protection of life and property and that is the reason. There have been threatening calls made." Was this before or after his involvement with the Alberta nationalist movement? "I did have the permit before the inordinate amount of publicity given to the independence movement in Alberta," he said. He handed me the dismantled gun, saying "Let me explain it to you. It's a double action, and that provides several very essential features. One, of course, it requires a long pull to fire the gun, so you don't fire by mistake or accident. Secondly, it's a double action and that ensures that I'll probably get a shot off if I'm lucky enough to get it out, without having to cock the hammer."

The second gun was a revolver. "Normally that would be within hand's reach," he said, "held by magnets in the office. Some revolvers you can pull through but most have to be cocked for each shot. This one is a single action which must be cocked. It's funny, people seem to take an unusual interest in the fact that I carry a gun, I don't know why." While he talked he constantly clicked, cocked and dismantled the weapons, finally, *reluctantly*?, putting them aside.

"There's this general feeling of alienation against the East," Mr. Harradence told me. "It goes back to the freight rates, tariffs, and I suppose the fact that the financial and political clout lies with Eastern Canada: 77 seats in Quebec, 88 seats in Ontario. And I think also the contempt — if there was a stinging or biting sort of contempt it wouldn't be so hard to take, but it's a casual contempt that they have — had, perhaps — for Western Canada and that has always been. But I don't think they [Albertans] felt anything could be done about it until we became a financial and economic power, which we are today.

"People in Edmonton and Calgary are complacent. They wouldn't support a movement of independence at this time. Wages are good, salaries are good, we're affluent, there are lineups to theaters, restaurants, travel agencies.

"There is that resentment, but with emotional ties to Canada. That's the only reason — the emotional ties — that holds the West in Confederation. Quite the opposite of Quebec. We can't afford to stay in Confederation and it's questionable if Quebec can afford to get out. However, there are several things that we have to appreciate. One is that the conventional reserves of petroleum run out about 1985 according to the government . . . . Now we have approximately a million and a half to a million and three quarters barrels of oil per day. That provides the government with 48 per cent of its income. When the conventional crude is gone, that's gone . . . it will be a catastrophic financial blow to the provincial government, and that's why Premier Lougheed is desperately trying to diversify.

"Now the export tax [which effectively prohibits Alberta from selling its oil in Canada at world market prices] is probably the most iniquitous tax that was ever imposed. Totally discriminatory. Not only is it discriminatory but it's contributing to the destruction of the oil industry in the world. You're subsidizing and encouraging a consumer to squander a diminishing natural resource, through the foreign exchange that's paid for foreign crude, and through the lack of revenue that comes to the government and to the oil industry by refusing to sell oil at the world price to the consumers in Ontario.

Harradence admitted that the tar sands and the heavy oil deposits may offer some relief but both are extremely expensive to produce. Prohibitively so, for the moment, and slow to get on-line production.

Back to separation which, if I understood him correctly, he doesn't seek for its own sake but thinks inevitable when Quebec secedes.

"Let me put this to you, my friend," he said, "and I use the word in a courteous sense. I believe it's been coming since 1759. We don't seek independence out here. If we could achieve recognition, if we could achieve the economic communities . . . I don't think we'd seek independence. But we can't as long as Quebec is part of the country: it contributes the 77 seats to back up Ontario. You know it's not by accident that Premier Bill Davis is desperate to keep Quebec in Confederation. Once Quebec goes we have him, because he needs us far more than we need him."

And there is absolutely no question in Milton Harradence's mind that Quebec will go. He is 55 years old, and was former Conservative leader of Alberta. He speaks only English — "the language of commerce, of technology," as he put it — and his exposure to the province of Quebec is limited to a ten-day legal seminar he once attended in Sherbrooke. But he sees the average French Canadian as elegant, with style, *elan*. "They have many wonderful racial characteristics and they see their language and their culture disappearing under the impact of North American technology. They're a minority here in Canada, and when you throw in the United States they're drowning, and if there's anything to them — and there's a hell of a lot to the French Canadians — they're not going to disappear without one hell of a struggle."

What then?

"Our view here is that we have no particular affection for Quebeckers any more than we have for the Italian Canadians, the Ukrainian Canadians, the German Canadians, the Dutch Canadians. You're an ethnic group and good luck to you, but you're on your own, don't expect us to help you. We'll trade with you. Why the hell wouldn't we? We trade with Red China, Cuba, Russia. But the trade must be of advantage to us and if it happens to be of advantage to you, that's the only way a deal is a good deal. But don't expect any accommodation from us and don't talk about using your St. Lawrence Seaway as a club. All it would take to straighten that out would be a summer cruise up the St. Lawrence by the U.S.S. *Tuscaloosa*."

Gunboat diplomacy, and not even one of our own gunboats. More and more the man disturbs me and I wonder how widespread this sort of thinking is. Certainly it would be rash for Quebec to fire ancient cannons at an American battleship. But then it would be diplomatically rash for an American battleship to "show the flag" to a country it has never even pretended to own. Ah, Mr. Harradence, you have a dangerous imagination.

And what of the rest of Canada?

"Ontario's going to have to completely revise its thinking. Your industrial complex can't survive on world markets. You can't produce in terms of world competition. . . . We don't mind making a certain contribution but you're going to pay world market prices for our oil.

"You must understand that the political and economic power has now shifted to Alberta. We'll consider your coming in with us [in the unlikely event that Alberta becomes a nation]. If you don't want that, good luck, you're on your own. We can make it. We've got everything. A gross domestic product of $15 billion." But Ontario residents will form a part of this new "Canada" only "if they're content to accept a subservient role — and that's very doubtful — and then I think we can maybe go on to achieve a certain destiny."

He's not too happy about British Columbia or Saskatchewan, either. Both have gone socialist "and that we can't tolerate. I'm a right-winger."

It's something I'd already figured out for myself. I had asked him if he felt no regret at all for the demise of what we know as Canada and he said that when he was young he was idealistic about the country, but that after the war, when the Leduc and Redwater oil deposits were discovered in Alberta "you wouldn't allow us the full Canadian market when we desperately needed it because you could get oil for a cent a gallon cheaper from Venezuela. We haven't forgotten that . . . it became very clear to me that the only reason we existed as a nation was to benefit Ontario and Quebec. . . . That being the case, it's no longer a nation, it's simply a convenience."

THE WESTERN National Association claims a membership of

about 500 people. Some of them, I suspect, are fairly influential people and they seem well organized. Harradence, for
example, gave me copies of research that was prepared at the
University of Calgary by Warren Blackman, Associate
Professor of Economics, entitled "The Cost of Confederation:
An Analysis of Costs to Alberta". Part One deals with
economic activity and Part Two, a separate volume, with intergovernmental transfer of funds. A third volume, prepared
by law faculty members of the University of Alberta, is called
"The Juridical Nature of Canadian Federalism: The Status of a
Province."

The two mimeographed volumes devoted to what Confederation costs Alberta are outrageously priced at $50 *each*
while the legal study is a more modest $25, and I suspect the
statistics and arguments contained are both logical and accurate, possibly even irrefutable. With no disrespect to the
authors, however, it seems to me that a friend of mine was right
when he told me, some years ago in Washington, D.C., that
history is seldom resolved with learned legal position papers or
policy statements but more likely with mail order guns and mail
box bombs and, occasionally, the will of the people.

If it ever came to a battle for western independence there'd
be little we could do about it. Peter Lougheed and A. Milton
Harradence, QC, aided perhaps by Bill Vander Zalm and Ed
Fleming (not to mention Victoria's Doug Christie) pitting their
strength against Pierre Elliott Trudeau? John Turner? Bill
Davis? Is there *no* leadership in English Canada today?

I DINED WITH friends that night who introduced me to a
French Canadian woman they knew, who had married a
Calgary pianist. Her name is Jocelyne and her husband is Miles
Jackson; both are in their early twenties. The music was loud
and conversation difficult but she told me she had lived on the
same street where Pierre La Porte was kidnapped. "It wasn't
fun," she said, but when, five years before at the age of 18, she
came out west it wasn't because of the Quebec revolution
building so much as age and her personal act of rebellion. "I

miss my family," she told me, "and I feel isolated, but I'm not going back." She married a westerner, she has become a westerner and her English improves each year.

Jocylene doesn't regard separatism in Quebec as "reality". How then did René Lévesque get elected? "He's been around for a long time," she said, "but to vote for him doesn't mean you want to be independent."

"Are you still *québécois* or are you a Calgarian?"

"I would say Calgarian. Yes. I'm planning to live for the rest of my life, like western, anyway. All Miles' contacts are here. When I met Miles I couldn't speak English very well and we practised on each other. But I'm going to teach the mother tongue to my children," she added firmly.

NEXT DAY I rose early and caught the bus for Edmonton, a three and a half hour run, and after an hour or two strolling through town I spent the day in my hotel room, working. The bus had been less than half full but I did meet Joanne Chemelinsky, a 22-year-old woman with her Bachelor of Education degree from the University of Edmonton. She's cheerful, pleasant and outspoken and she has visited Quebec. But when I asked what she and her family thought of Lévesque and the prospect of separation she seemed to withdraw. Her father, she said, "is a real Archie Bunker on the subject." He's a Ukrainian Canadian farmer and she learned to speak Ukrainian as a second language at school. "But it didn't help me much in Quebec," she added ruefully.

On Saturday, May 28, I left the flatlands of Alberta for the even flatter lands of Saskatchewan, first with a seven and a half hour run to Saskatoon, 328 miles distant, and, then, after a brief stopover, a three hour run to Regina. It was on this leg of the journey that I found myself sitting with an 18-year-old girl named Laurie Anderson. Actually I'd been across the aisle from her but a married couple got on the bus and there were no double seats left so I moved over, somewhat reluctantly; it had been a gruelling if scenic ride and I wasn't feeling very talkative. But sometimes traveling by bus you get lucky when you least expect it.

Laurie Anderson is one of those rare and charming people who like other people; she gave me a friendly smile and told me she was going home to her father's farm just north of Regina. She had just graduated from a course in cosmetology in Saskatoon and had a job waiting for her in Regina. She chatted about her father, a third-generation Scandinavian Canadian, the problems of trying to support a half-section farm and how they had to ship their beef to Toronto for butchering. Her father survives with a medium-sized printing business in Regina, because you can't exist on a half-section farm on the Prairies; you need at least a full section or a section and a half. A section, of course, is a square mile, and it seemed to me that when I was covering the farm beat for the *Orillia Packet and Times* back in the mid-1950s (it was my first newspaper and my first job) a section of land was quite a respectable farm. You might never get rich but you'd never go hungry, either. And as I listened, I wanted more and more to meet this man so I invited myself out for a visit. Laurie said she'd call her dad when we got to the bus terminal to make sure it was all right. I said I'd rent a car. The farm was about fifteen miles out of town.

Rudy Anderson was agreeable but dubious. There'd been a lot of rain — some serious flooding in several neighboring communities — and the road might not be passable. I scoffed at that and told Laurie "just ask him what time I'm to be there."

And that is how I learned a great deal about gumbo soil, a distant cousin of quicksand. It goes down about fifty feet in that area and you don't really use the steering wheel when it's wet, except to try to stay in the tractor ruts because if you get out of them you may be stuck for a month. And you have to keep your speed up, too, to at least thirty-five or forty miles an hour which is nerve-racking when you can't steer properly. And of course I got lost so it took me about an hour and a half to travel fifteen miles but I made it eventually.

Gumbo is also a very fine soil and when there's a dry spell it blows from one field to the next, burying farm machinery completely. But it will grow wheat. Although why anyone would want to I don't know. I'd sooner play roulette. The work is easier and the odds of success, I suspect, more favorable.

Rudy Anderson was cleaning the cattle barn when I arrived. He keeps about fifteen head, about 125 chickens, has about 130 acres of wheat and barley and I asked him what that meant in terms of income.

"Very poor," he said. "You could never make a living off a half-section, you'd have to go to a section or a section and a half and then you'd be looking at an income of about $12,000, maybe $15,000. That's net."

What about the costs? Well that can vary quite a lot, he told me. There's the equipment. "You go out and buy a new self-propelled combine and you're looking at anywhere from $30,000 to $50,000 just for the combine. Look at a new tractor and you're looking at anywhere from $12,000 to $50,000 and there's the tillage equipment, an average sized 16-foot discer, you're looking at $4,000. You can run into anywhere from $100,000 to $500,000 or more. On a three-section farm, I know some people who have a big unit — four-wheel drive and two 16-foot discers behind it and the whole unit is worth $80,000."

Trouble is that what has to be done has to be done quickly on a wheat farm. That means discers to aerate the soil before planting and the planting can't wait so the discer has to be adequate, powerful tractors, combines that can mow and bale the wheat and get the job done before it starts to rain. So you're talking about $100,000 worth of equipment with which you may earn a net income of $12,000 to $15,000 and that, of course, doesn't take the price of the land and buildings into consideration. But Rudy wasn't through with me yet.

"Then you've got your operating expenses," he said. "In the spring, what it costs for your seed. I've sowed 130 acres and I bought weed control spray — I spent $1,100 on chemicals alone. Wheat and barley. Right now barley's around $2.65 a bushel and wheat's around $2.57 a bushel. I sowed a bushel and a half to the acre so you're looking at another $3 to $3.50 per acre [a total somewhere between $390 and $455]. Crop insurance cost me $285 last year. Then there's your diesel fuel, which isn't cheap either, going up five per cent, then another three or four cents in July, and another three or four cents every six months for the next two years. Whether the price of grain will go up I don't know. Then there's your harvesting expenses . . . it's a gamble, you're strictly dependent on the weather."

Rudy Anderson bought the farm three years ago; he'd had a heart operation in 1973 and figured the exercise would be good for him. Business pressure, he said. His printing business has about fifteen employees. "Walk a block a day, they say. You don't have to worry about walking a block a day if you're looking after a half-section." He gets up at six o'clock in the morning to milk the cows, gets to his office in Regina about nine o'clock and works until six, and then he comes home to work on the farm until dark. And on weekends. "It's not an easy sort of life," he said, "but it's a different life. If you're doing one thing all the time it becomes sort of a bore."

Ella, his wife, is of German descent, and there's Laurie and a younger sister, Janice, in high school, and an older son, Les (and his wife, Margaret), both living on the farm but Les is studying business administration and accounting in town. Rudy farms because he likes it, because he was born to it, and because he figured it would be good for his health. He talks easily, with wry amusement more than bitterness at the various things he has to contend with. Like selling beef.

"You ship the beef down to Toronto and you pay the freight, and they process it and ship it back to you, adding the freight to the over-the-counter price — cured meats, sausages and so on. So we pay the freight going down and we pay the freight coming back here again."

Shipping beef on the hoof costs seven to ten cents a pound for an animal that may weigh anywhere from 700 to 1,800 pounds. On a 1,000 pound animal, Rudy says, "you're probably looking at 600 pounds of dressed beef. About 60 per cent of hoof beef is dressed meat. We pay the shipping charges on hoof meat." And he added, "You'll find the beef prices in Toronto are as cheap or cheaper than they are here."

Rudy's all right. He's got a printing business in Regina to keep him solvent, a farm to keep him alive and a sense of humor to make it all worthwhile. All he has to worry about is rain, and there's not much point farming if you're the type to

brood about rain. There's either too much or too little. A few
months earlier they were praying for rain. A few days ago they
got four inches in a single day at nearby Lumsden, two years
ago an overnight fall on Rudy's farm dropped six inches and
turned it into a lake. Another year there was a dust storm and
his water trough disappeared. Hell, he even had to dig to find
the *tops* of his plow and harrow.

The rain has to come at the right time, too, at planting time,
so the seeds will germinate (but not so much that they will rot),
maybe an inch or two every two or three weeks until July, and
then enough to fill the kernels out. The normal head of wheat
will grow four rows of seeds and if you get the right moisture
you may get more rows. "I've seen where they had *eight* rows,
and you're increasing your yield considerably."

If you don't get rain the kernels will dry out and shrivel and
if you do, and the crop looks good, a half-hour hailstorm can
hammer it into the ground and off you go to collect your crop
insurance.

OK, I'm a city boy, but it sounds like guaranteed ulcers to
me. I'd have to take up Zen or something.

We had "lunch" and Ella filled me to the sleeping point
with a rich beef stew. She said the meat was tough (it wasn't) so
it must have been Ontario beef. And salad and bread and
Saskatoon berries, a cross between cranberries and blueberries.
I mentioned my interview with Milt Harradence and my interest
in other people's reactions to René Lévesque and Rudy said
"Oh yes, we hear lots about Quebec and about making Alberta
a country. Being in the business world you meet a lot of people
and you get a lot of different feelings.

"The western people feel Easterners don't care about them
and I suppose Easterners feel the same way about us. I don't
know, I've never been East to find out. I do know a lot of
people out here feel it would be best to separate the four
western provinces. We've got our own seashore, we've got the
United States. But I think a lot of them don't realize the
problems that would arise. . . . Eventually I think you'd have a
lot more friction than you have now," What a man like Rudy
Anderson doesn't need, in an already complicated life, is a

whole new set of international borders, customs, import and export duties, and so on.

Does he think Quebec will go?

"No, I think a lot of people — Anglo Saxons too, from what I can understand here — they voted for the *Parti Québécois* because they were sort of fed up with the federal government and figured Lévesque would take a harder line on certain things. I think if it comes to a referendum that they'll vote against it. . . .

"And you can't really blame Alberta or Saskatchewan because I remember when they made those huge discoveries of oil, set up oil wells and bought a pipeline, the Trans Canada Pipeline, and we couldn't export oil to the East, to Ontario and Quebec and the Maritimes because they were getting it cheaper from Arabia and Ecuador and Venezuela. They said 'We don't want your oil,' so a lot of it was exported into Minneapolis but every once in a while they'd have enough oil and they'd shut us off. I think this is the background to the whole problem with Alberta and Saskatchewan because of lot of those people, they haven't forgotten, you know. They haven't forgotten."

That, from a thoughtful and reasonable man who has no interest at all in splitting Canada apart. The same arguments used by western separatists.

The sun was shining when I left, late in the afternoon, and the roads had dried out a bit so I didn't have as much trouble. Nor did I get lost. When I returned the rented car, I parked it carefully beside a truck so they couldn't see it from the rental office window. Silly thing to do, but that little car looked awful. There must have been a half ton of gumbo stuck to it. Back to my hotel to type up my notes and transcript and eventually to bed. The car rental man who drove me back to my hotel told me there'd been a shooting there about a year before. He'd been present and had had to testify in court. Some guy had just walked into the bar and shot up the place, wounding four people. "Odd," he said, "it's a fairly high class place, too." I don't know if anyone was killed, I wasn't really listening. I was wondering how long I'd last in Western Canada before I got bloody angry. I don't have Rudy Anderson's gentle equanimity.

Next day I stayed at the Blackstone Hotel in Yorkton and Olga Krepakevich was telling me more of the same. She and her husband Victor own a half-section farm just outside town but they're leasing it this year and she was working four days a week at the hotel. "We paid $35,000 a quarter for it," she said. "Seventy thousand dollars. And then $25,000 for a tractor — we've got maybe $100,000 invested and can't make a living off it." She talked of farmers who couldn't sell their wheat because the granaries were still full and said she knew one man who was making $1,400 a month interest payments.

It had been a seven and a half hour run to Yorkton; I'd got a late start, they'd rolled up the sidewalks for the night and Olga very kindly made me a chicken sandwich. "Quebec?" she said, "Let 'em go. But they don't have the right, and if they go, why not all the others?"

She's a kindly woman who, with her husband, owns a farm worth $100,000 and they can't make a living from it so they're trying a year in town, and she's working as receptionist at a $12-a-night hotel. "The kids won't let us sell it," she said. "It's good land."

A FEW DAYS later I would read a newspaper interview with Emmett Hall, retired Supreme Court Justice, 79-year-old author of the government's study of the nation's railways and the proposed abandonment of 6,300 miles of track out of a total western system of 20,000 miles. Hall spent the first twelve years of his life in Quebec but now lives in Saskatoon. "Speaking as a Westerner," he told a reporter from Toronto, "the matter [of Quebec] doesn't have the notoriety and concern expressed elsewhere. The West has so many problems of its own that it views Ontario and Quebec together as the ones who benefit from Confederation."

He claimed that Confederation isn't endangered but added that he would like to see a commitment on the part of the federal government toward building up the West and the Maritimes, by locating secondary industries closer to the sources of materials they use. More disturbing words from yet another thoughtful, well-respected man.

ANOTHER LONG run next day to Portage La Prairie and a more or less wasted day. I was beginning to weary of buses, prairies and people so I scribbled some notes, quit when I realized they were illegible and went to bed.

A SHORT RUN to Winnipeg next morning and I didn't even look for a hotel. I went to a pay phone in the bus terminal and called Barney Lamm, in Gimli. He roared a welcome in my ear and asked where I was. "Meet me at the airport at three o'clock," he ordered. "At the private aircraft area, they'll tell you where. I've got to come into town anyway and you can spend the night here and we'll have ourselves some steak."

Damn it, it's great to find a friend in the middle of an endless journey when you're tired and feeling very much alone among some twenty-two million people. In thirty seconds my world had changed. I was going to take a few days off.

I MET BARNEY and Marion Lamm several years ago at the Grassy Narrows Indian Reserve, forty miles out of Kenora, Ontario. I'd been assigned to do a magazine article on the mercury poisoning which had destroyed the Indians' economy and devastated their lives. It's been well documented, both in countless articles and several books. One year the welfare payments to the Grassy Narrows people came to a paltry $10,000; the following year, because of the belated discovery that the fish they were making their living from were poisoned, the figure rose by a factor of ten and both Grassy Narrows and the neighboring White Dog reserves were ruined.

Barney and Marion Lamm had operated a fantastically popular and financially successful fishing resort at Ball Lake and annually employed more than a hundred Indians as guides and staff. It's probably fair to say the Indians helped make him a wealthy man, just as he — for twenty years — gave them a solid and dependable income. A symbiotic relationship. And the Indians respected and liked Barney; their eyes would light up and they'd smile when he entered a room. He was the man who made things happen.

The Lamms closed Ball Lake Lodge because the fish their wealthy American guests were catching and eating were contaminated with mercury, dumped in the English-Wabigoon river system by a pulp mill. That's what Barney says, anyway. My own view is that he was at least as concerned about the Indian guides he employed. A tourist can eat a few contaminated fish without seriously damaging himself but it had become ominously clear to everyone but the Ontario Government that the daily ritual of the shore dinner was slowly killing the Indians.

Barney also has a thriving air transport business based in Gimli, north of Winnipeg; he had a policy of making his aircraft available to any responsible writer interested in the mercury poisoning and the Minamata disease symptoms and he personally flew me to the reserve, to his lodge, to White Dog reserve, opening a lot of doors. Often merely being seen with him would break down the barriers and Indians who had been openly suspicious and hostile to the tall, strange, surly looking writer from the south would seek me out to talk. The Lamms are gracious, warm people and I looked forward to seeing them again.

Sharp at three that afternoon he sauntered into the airport office and we flew in one of his Cessnas, to his home, the former commandant's quarters at what was once Gimli Air Force Base, now becoming an aircraft-oriented industrial park. Steaks were barbecued, wine and conversation flowed. They were leaving early next morning to attend their daughter's graduation from high school in the States and would return in a couple of days. I was to remain there, get caught up on sleep and work, relax and be comfortable. Here were the keys to the Cherokee Jeep and yes, he'd certainly tape an interview with me when he returned.

I spent two nights there, luxuriating in the privacy, typing reams of notes, driving into the town of Gimli when I was too lazy to cook for myself, and when the Lamms came back Barney and I sat down and he told me about the people he knew in that corner of the province. His clients — mostly American executives or fishermen — didn't know much about Quebec, he said, nor about Canada either, for that matter. Their attitude seemed generally to be "Let 'em go, if they want to," but the natives, Canadians of Icelandic and Ukrainian descent, had a curious combination of apathy and hostility. "The Icelanders are pretty angry," he said.

As for Quebec, he doesn't feel a referendum would pass. "I think they're using it for all it's worth. I don't think even Lévesque is really interested in separating the country. They're going to get all the goodies they can out of this movement.

"But there *is* a lot of western separatism. I think Lougheed's probably got a better chance of separating than Lévesque has. He could make a go of it. I haven't really considered it a serious enough problem to get into. I don't know whether we'd go in with them or not. Manitoba is a poor province, you know, but unemployment is low, the lowest of any province in Canada by a couple of percentage points. You don't have the influx of people coming into Manitoba. The population is only about a million, and half of that is in Winnipeg.

"I heard on the radio the other day that our employment is going to get even better, unemployment will be maybe two and a half per cent lower than the rest of the provinces, the minimum wage is probably the highest of any province and they're talking about overtime and raising the minimum wage to $3 an hour as of this fall.

"This is what's hurting the country, there's no productivity at that kind of wage. It's the trend all over the country. We have people, real good people, and they'll come and say 'I'd like to take the summer off, would you give me a letter saying it's kind of seasonal work, that you'll need me in the fall but lay me off now so I can collect unemployment insurance?' One of my mechanics came to me saying 'Gee, I'd like to play golf all summer, if you'd just give me a letter. . . .'"

I asked if people were looking for work, like the Calgary teenagers, rather than jobs and he said no. "We did see that in Ontario, in Kenora. But mostly the people we find looking for a job are really looking for a long term job. The Indians are probably more sincere about really working than most. And we draw from the farming communities. They know what work is. The old man has kicked them out of bed to milk the cows before they go to school. We find that a farm background makes the best employee, he'll do a little extra. . . ."

I said my farewells, hopped into Barney's jeep ("Just leave it at the airport, I'll pick it up later.") and drove to Gimli to talk to Joe Arnason, a craggy-faced, dour 62-year-old Icelandic furniture dealer. If he's typical, the Icelanders are even more dour than the Scots. Maybe it's because they come from further north.

He greeted me hospitably enough but without rising or smiling, reminding me more than anything else of a New Englander. Sort of an I-don't-like-or-dislike-you-what-do-you-want attitude. He had a deeply lined face and a handsome shock of snow white hair and I took an immediate liking to the man. He told me he's first generation: his father immigrated and homesteaded and it was a hard life. "That's why I left the farm. Too much work for nothing." One of his seven brothers now operates it, a three-quarter section farm.

He told me he found it very depressing, what's being done to Canada. He's been to Montreal and to Russia, Mexico and Iceland. "I'm disappointed the English haven't put a stop to it. The Prime Minister and Cabinet are French so we're governed by a few radicals who have misused their power. Nobody will give us good government because everybody caters to the French vote. They govern to get the next vote; it's disgraceful! There's no *true* government."

We've become a second-rate nation, he said. "But the French are good people, I've nothing against them. Just that bunch of radicals."

Arnason used to be president of the Gimli Chamber of Commerce and served, for a time, as director-at-large for the Manitoba Chamber. Pretty soon Harold Dalman joined us.

He's the current president of Gimli Chamber of Commerce, a 59-year-old third generation Icelander who runs a camp for crippled children a few miles north of Gimli. Arnason's son and daughter were in and out of the office, sometimes bringing coffee, sometimes riffling through papers stacked on his desk, sometimes muttering approval of something one of their elders had said. The conversation became a bit disjointed, more like a hot stove session than an interview, but my notes are clear and I've rearranged them for the sake of clarity and continuity. Here is what I learned.

The Interlake Country — the land between Lakes Manitoba and Winnipeg — was settled originally by Icelanders. They naturally gravitated toward lake country similar to what they had left behind. Similarly the Ukrainians tended to settle on the prairies, which probably reminded them of the steppes. "Interlake," said Dalman, "is a prime part of Canadian culture. It *is* Western Canada. Settled first by Icelanders, then Polish, Norwegians, Swedes — a real good cross-section. We were all ethnics, afraid to speak to each other, afraid to intermarry. But we all went to one type of school and that helped Interlake. Now we call ourselves Canadians. The Icelanders were a dull, drab people and we were affected by eastern Europeans. The Ukrainians brought us color. Made us a more interesting people than the dull, drab, stern original settlers. Honest people with a strict moral outlook.

"The Icelander would paint his house white, with no trimming. The eastern Europeans painted their homes with color. They gave *us* color. The Icelanders became better farmers because of our proximity to the Ukrainians and we taught them fishing . . ."

I was moved by this little history lesson. Arnason didn't seem to disagree with any of it but he switched sharply back to Quebec, saying "I don't think they want to separate, they want a welfare state. That I don't mind, but don't spread it through the rest of Canada . . . Canada is my country. Keep Canada for Canadians — anybody that speaks English. We should have an English Canadian culture." I was more than amused. Arnason speaks English masterfully but he's got an accent you could cut with a butter knife. "Canada's too good a country to be torn apart by a few radicals," he continued. "Put 'em all on welfare for five years and teach them English."

Dalman said that the British North America Act "said one thing, they could keep their language, schools and religion and use French in Parliament — it never said Canada should be bilingual. You can't take a chunk out of the country, and a pretty big chunk, too. . . . Trudeau was an early day hippie who became an undersecretary. You send a man to school for fifty years and you've got an educated fool . . . we're not being ripped off by the East but by Confederation. . . ."

I left Gimli with my head spinning. Bigots? No way. Opinionated old buggers, maybe, and refreshingly blunt. And Dalman runs a camp for crippled children. Funny they didn't mention the Red River Valley and how the French had settled and homesteaded the land less than a hundred miles south. But those two Icelanders, their attitude toward Quebec seemed more defensive than offensive. And you can take that either way you like.

I DROVE TO Winnipeg and booked a room at the Mall Hotel, which is right on top of the bus terminal. Shower and food and back to the jeep, heading for St. Boniface: I wanted to talk to Georges Forest, badly.

In British Columbia, in Alberta, in Saskatchewan and in the back of a furniture store in Gimli, Manitoba, I'd heard tales of this lunatic who was suing the City of Winnipeg over a traffic ticket because it was printed in English, and who intended to single-handedly force Winnipeg to become an officially bilingual city. Alas, I met no lunatics on my 5,000-mile odyssey. (Well, maybe *one*, and I'm naming no names. I'd get sued for sure.) In fact the real lunatic was myself, for thinking I could come to grips with Canada simply by traveling across its breadth by bus. It will take me the rest of my life. It's a big country and there just aren't the stereotypes there are in the United States (and maybe not there, either). Stereotypes are very reassuring to journalists because you can generalize about them. You can't generalize about Canadians — at least I can't.

Georges Forest wasn't home, he was off playing ball with one of his kids but should be back soon. I said I'd wait and sat on his porch. After a while his other children must have decided I looked harmless and invited me in to wait in the living room.

St. Boniface was a city, once, essentially a French city. Today it's just part of Winnipeg, a suburb of about 45,000 people of whom roughly one third are French, have French names, French origins. People likes Georges Forest.

"I was born here in Manitoba," he told me when he eventually arrived. "I am now 53 years of age. My father came from Bonaventure, Quebec; my mother is of local stock. Her mother was Métis. I ran for Parliament as a Social Credit candidate the year of the Trudeau landslide and I ran that fall for the last term of office of the Mayor of St. Boniface. [He lost both.]

There are about a million French Canadians living outside of Quebec and they are, most of them, concerned about the implications of René Lévesque's victory on their lives and on their cultural rights. Wisely so, because separation aside, it seems reasonable to assume that the more French Quebec becomes, the more English the rest of Canada will become and it is this fear that drives men like Georges Forest.

"In 1971 we were faced with Unicity," he told me. "This was Mayor Stephen Juba's dream. 'Give me St. Boniface,' he said many years ago, 'and I will make of it a little Paree'".

"Commercial. Place Pigalle. New Orleans. *Tourist trap*." Georges Forest fairly spat the word out. Thwarted politically he decided to be whatever nuisance he could to the anglicization of St. Boniface and in this he has been moderately and expensively successful. Sometimes it is the little things that hurt the most. In Calgary it was the "casual contempt". In St. Boniface, in 1960, Nicole Forest was born and her parents received a congratulatory letter signed by "your Mayor, Stephen Juba". "Mayor of Winnipeg, yes," growled Forest. But not for another eleven years would he become Forest's mayor. The City of St. Boniface had its own.

He also did some positive things. Forest was instrumental in organizing the Festival du Voyageur in 1970. He dressed himself as St. Jean Baptiste Lagimodière, who, in 1815, walked to Montreal to warn Lord Selkirk that the Red River colony was in peril. His wife dressed as Marieanne Gaboury, the first white woman to establish a household in the Red River Valley.

But on February 7th, 1976, Georges Forest parked his car in front of his insurance office and forgot about it, and a policeman tagged it. A small matter, just a $5 overtime parking tag. The parking tag, however, was printed in English and that, of course, was intolerable.

"There were three official languages in Manitoba before it became a province in 1870," Forest told me. "English, French, and either Ojibway or Cree and nothing has been done to change that. Legislation was brought before the House in 1910 and passed, but the Lieutenant Governor never signed it. And the City of Winnipeg Act, section 80, subsection iii, states that all communications sent or demands made [in St. Boniface] . . . shall be in English and French." The key phrase was "the rendering of a service" and Judge J.S. Walker ruled that this was not a service of the police or of the city but of the court. Therefore the City of Winnipeg Act did not apply. Five dollars and costs, a total of $14.90.

Actually they do have bilingual traffic tickets in St. Boniface. The cop had simply run out of them. Now at this point, not being versed in law but, as a journalist, reasonably competent to smell a can of worms when it has been opened, had I been sitting on the bench I would have dismissed the case on some technicality or other, reprimanded the cop and prayed that M. Forest would go home. But Judge Walker, perhaps mindful of Lord Mansfield's famous quotation of the 1770s, "Let Justice be done, even though the Heavens fall," ruled as he saw fit.

So far Georges Forest has spent "a few thousands" of his own money plus $5,000 raised by supporters (including thirty contributions from Anglophones) on his appeal, and if that fails there is no question that he'll carry it to the Supreme Court.

It all reminds me of a case nearly twenty years ago, when a

young law student challenged the wording of a city's no parking signs *and won*. The city, at vast expense, had to repaint all its no parking signs. Again, not being versed in the law, I'm afraid I would have thrown the case out of court, called the mayor and told him either to rewrite the law or repaint the signs on a gradual basis.

It's not that I disagree with Georges Forest; I'm with him. I just can't see calling in the Supreme Court when a little common sense would be just as effective and a hell of a lot cheaper. The policeman should have been reprimanded for running out of bilingual parking tags and the matter dropped. Now, of course, with the election of Lévesque and the threat of a referendum, a certain emotional symbolism has come into play.

"Lévesque," says Forest, "is one of the best things that ever happened to Canada. I suspect secession is likely if there is no sincere response from the rest of Canada. . .

"I'm just the guy that's putting the bell on the cat."

T HE NEXT MORNING, Eugene Giguere said, "Well, I guess like most people in Canada I think it's a question of uncertainty. What's going to happen to French Canadians outside Quebec? I myself was born in Quebec but I've been living in Manitoba for twenty years."

Eugene Giguere is director of the Centre Culturel Franco-Manitoban, an impressive establishment on Boul. Provencher, in St. Boniface. It was built for $100,000 in 1974, paid for by the Province of Manitoba. The institution exists solely to further French culture and language in Manitoba, through a varied program of classes, theatrical productions and so on.

"My own feeling," Giguere told me, "is that Lévesque doesn't want separation, I think he wants more power for the province of Quebec. We have to understand that Quebec is not a province like the others. . .Eighty per cent of the province is French and has to have special status, and the only way they can do it is to amend the constitution. Not strictly in favor of Quebec, but the federal government has to change.

"The reaction here is not fear but uncertainty. We would

lose everything. Lévesque said at the University of Manitoba that there was only one place in Canada for a French Canadian and that was in the province of Quebec. My wife is from Manitoba. She learned French the hard way, in the 1930s. There was no French taught in the schools. If they did, it was under the table.

"There are two great leaders, Pierre Trudeau and René Lévesque. They're both from the same schools and have ideas. One of these days they're going to crash together and that crash will be to the good of the country. Something has to be done for all the provinces, not only Quebec. Quebec is asking for language and culture. Other provinces are talking about transport, energy. But all the provinces will benefit from that crash. We'll have to bring the constitution home to Canada and the ministers of all the provinces will have to sit down and come together. It's going to be hard. They're both stubborn but they'll have to sit down together . . ."

THURSDAY, JUNE 2, a short run of two and a half hours carries me out of the prairies and into my native Ontario. At 5:30 p.m. we passed a sign informing us that we had just passed the longitudinal center of Canada — 96 degrees, so many minutes, so many seconds.

And so very many miles. It took a minute or so for the meaning of that sign to sink in, which is why I didn't get the number of minutes and seconds of longitude. I was thinking of Eugene Giguere, hearing his voice in my mind asking doubtfully: "If we have Italian classes in Toronto, why not French elsewhere? Or even Icelandic, or Ukrainian — wherever there is a demand?

Why not indeed? And why can I so seldom agree or disagree with the people I meet on this trip? It is not my nature to be ambivalent but the country is too big, and there are too many reasonable people in it who disagree with each other.

ONTARIO
Fat Cats Speak English

D RIED BLOOD stained the sidewalk in front of Ted's Cafe when I arrived in Kenora, and if the abrupt emergence from prairie flatland to the rocky pine forests of northern Ontario had made me homesick a few hours earlier, the harsh reality of this troubled and, I think, guilt-ridden town put me in an even more dismal frame of mind. There's blood on the streets of Kenora every day, a visible symbol of despair shared, in varying degrees, by some seven or eight thousand Indians whose Treaty 3 reserves surround the town of less than ten thousand people.

The affable off-duty shopkeeper who paused to chat didn't help either. He was a portly little man with that genial, slightly pompous attitude that smalltowners often use both as badge of belonging and as a distancing mechanism. Small town geniality can be deceptive; it isn't always a sign of friendliness but can mask suspicion of a stranger who is clearly not a tourist. It was the shopkeeper who pointed out the bloodstained sidewalk, almost with a sense of defensive pride, and he carefully avoided using the word "Indian" as he described the hoodlums who had knifed each other the night before, just as I now avoid the word "bigot" to describe him. It's too harsh, and the problems facing what was once a charming, thriving northern Ontario fishing resort town are unresolved and likely will remain so for years to come.

As the bus entered town we'd passed Husky the Muskie, a forty-foot-tall fiberglass replica of the king of fighting gamefish, carrying the ironic inscription "HELP PREVENT WATER POLLUTION". It was early evening and after checking my bags at the Kenricia Hotel, I ambled down toward the waterfront. When the shopkeeper accosted me, I wasn't feeling conversational and tried to discourage him by turning down a residential street but he came along, chattering amiably about the weather, and the fishing. Suddenly a carload of young Indians, perhaps in their early twenties, came and stopped in the middle of the road. The door opened and a man leapt out of the passenger seat, darted across the sidewalk and front lawn of a fine old home somewhat in need of paint but a reminder nonetheless of better, more affluent days. The young man knelt at the base of a clump of lilac bushes, reached into the shrubbery and extracted one, then another forty-ounce bottle of red wine. He quickly returned to the car which sped off before he'd had time to close the door. It took about thirty seconds for this to happen, and in that moment my acquaintance's face turned black.

No more talk of fishing and weather, no more pretensions. He let loose a stream of invective against drunken Indians spoiling the town and I found myself angry with the young Indian for giving the shopkeeper the opening he seemed to crave. The youth had not yet been drinking — although that, obviously, was about to change — and he displayed about as much decorum as any young man might do with a case of beer, a car full of friends and an evening ahead.

Kenora, says Mayor Udo Romstedt, is fed up with its "drunken Indian" image, fed up with "outsiders coming in here to show us our social problems. Nobody comes with a solution. I *know* the problem, and they're caused by a handful of problem drinkers, all of them visible on the streets."

A federal government worker who has been involved with

Indian communities across Canada told me he regards Grassy Narrows and White Dog, the two reserves closest to Kenora, as among the most degraded and demoralized in the land. Well, I'd visited Kenora several times and once spent a week living in the back of the Roman Catholic Church on the Grassy Narrows reserve. None of this surprised me.

Several years ago I had been assigned to write a magazine article on the mercury problem. After fruitless interviews at Queen's Park I had visited both reserves where the Indians talked to me out of their innate sense of courtesy. But they were clearly less than pleased at the intrusion of yet another southern reporter into their personal lives with the reminder that some of them would likely die from eating poisoned fish at the traditional "shore dinners" with the tourists they guided. I'd had fairly brutal interviews with two or three of the guides whose blood samples showed dangerously high levels of mercury, listening as they described their symptoms, and probing none too gently into their bleak, possibly brief futures. It was an unpleasant assignment and I recall observing that the symptoms of mercury poisoning or Minamata disease are similar to those of drunkenness: slurred conversation, lurching and stumbling, tunnel vision and so on. If you see an Indian staggering along the streets of Kenora you can't be certain whether he's drunk or sick or both; in any event they have much to drink about.

The mercury comes from two sources. It was used in mining operations a century ago and there are traces of it in most northern lakes. But the bulk of it comes from pulp and paper mills and recently, after years of litigation, a provincial court at Thunder Bay found Reed Paper Ltd. "conditionally guilty" of five charges of polluting the Wabigoon river system on which the Indians had depended.

Barney Lamm was the first to close down his luxury fishing resort on Ball Lake, refusing to lure his wealthy American guests — who had been returning regularly for twenty years which were profitable to Barney and to the more than one hundred Indians he employed — to catch and eat poisoned fish. One or two more lodge owners followed but others remained open, claiming, as were provincial government politicians and government-employed doctors, that the link between mercury-tainted fish and deforming and often fatal cases of Minamata disease had yet to be proven. And of course the cynical and possibly accurate argument was that it would take a courageous and perhaps suicidal government to close down fishing in an area that depended so heavily on high-spending fishermen from the United States. Instead, the government ordered the Indians to stop fishing in the polluted system but refused to close down the waterway to all fishermen.

It was a terrible blow to the whole region, but particularly to Kenora, and tempers were short. Barney Lamm, a classic example of Ibsen's "Enemy of the People", moved his family to Gimli, Manitoba, leaving a few Indians to prevent deterioration of the buildings and equipment at his million-dollar Ball Lake Lodge. Many of the townspeople were glad to see him go, but a few realized that Kenora had lost one of its chief benefactors and boosters. In his place came hundreds of unemployed Indians, pooling their resources for the $40 cab ride to the town and drinking their sorrows away, paying for cheap red wine with welfare cheques. When the money ran out, almost any substitute would do. One winter six Indians, ignoring the skull and crossbones symbol clearly printed on the container, died by drinking antifreeze.

Shortly after I returned home from my cross-country tour I noticed a headline in the *Toronto Star*: "Don't eat Huntsville area trout". The accompanying article particularly cautioned that "pregnant women, nursing mothers and children under 15" were exceptionally vulnerable. The provincial environment ministry had tested trout at mercury levels as high as 10 parts per million while "the maximum permissible safe level is .5 parts per million." That's close to a thousand miles closer to Queen's Park than Kenora. Maybe when it gets down to Lake Simcoe the government will be forced to act. Meanwhile, yet another segment of our population has become alienated and distrustful of government. Simultaneously we have managed to destroy two of our lucrative natural resources, commercial fishing, and our tourist industry.

Indians in the Mackenzie Delta have been arming themselves and threatening to establish a Dene Nation if their land
claims aren't met. Prairie Indians have also armed themselves
and there have been shooting incidents, some fatal, over
hunting restrictions. Indians in northern Quebec, who learned
to speak English from the Hudson's Bay traders and Anglican
priests long before the land was ceded to the province as
Nouveau Québec, are threatening secession over René
Lévesque's language bill. The Treaty 3 Indians of northwestern
Ontario can hardly declare themselves a nation, but can
Canada itself survive with so much alienation spread so
diversely yet so evenly across the country?

I disentangled myself from my Kenora companion and
wandered back to the cocktail lounge of the Kenricia Hotel, a
gathering place where I hoped to pick up some local gossip. The
Davis election was approaching its climax and having seen Leo
Bernier's "More Work To Be Done" campaign posters I
wondered how the newly appointed Minister of Northern
Affairs was doing.

As soon as my eyes became accustomed to the darkness (it
was still sunny outside) I was able to recognize the man who
was laughing and calling my name: Barney Lamm, sitting with
one of his pilots. "John," he commanded, "come have a
drink." I joined him with considerable misgivings, knowing I
had just succeeded in alienating at least half the people in the
room; I could *feel* it. Barney spends a lot of time in Kenora
still, keeping in touch with the Indians he knows so well,
recognizing in them a potential political power bloc, and
lobbying with the more progressive citizens in town. He has a
multi-million dollar suit in the works against the provincial
government for losses in revenue resulting from closing the Ball
Lake Lodge, and he also has intricate schemes for reopening it
someday that would require both political support and
government funds from the same politicians — men like Leo
Bernier — with whom he has been doing battle for six or seven
years. Barney is a complex man, a natural entrepreneur full of
intricate and generally lucrative schemes which benefit all
concerned. The Indians of Grassy Narrows made him a wealthy

man by guiding and cossetting his lodge guests. In turn, they could count on three or four thousand dollars income each season which, combined with a bit of hunting and trapping and the autumn migration of gamefowl provided a pretty good standard of living. Alcoholism was low and they had little need of welfare.

Barney also has a dose of the impatience of the self-made man and some find him blunt-spoken and abrasive in his business dealings, although even his enemies swear to his honesty and ultimate fairness.

I sat with him and twitted him about his political intrigues. I knew what he was doing in Kenora and I knew he didn't want to talk about it. He was attempting to organize an Indian protest vote against the government. It wouldn't hurt Leo Bernier, but it would be an unmistakable message to Queen's Park. He smiled inscrutably and nodded to a cluster of tables nearby, where about a dozen clean-cut businessmen were doing more talking than drinking. "Bernier's boys," he said. "They won't like your sitting with me."

He left as soon as he'd finished his ginger ale, a tip-off that he'd got himself a charter. There were several small forest fires in the area and he'd offered to fly in some supplies. Well, when your cover's blown you simply brazen your way through. I approached the cluster of tables and, in the sudden, small-town silence asked "Is Doug Johnson here?"

"Who wants him?" came the reply, neither friendly nor hostile.

"I'm a writer from Toronto," I said, "and he's the president of your Chamber of Commerce. He's had a bit of publicity in Toronto and I wanted to ask him some questions." That broke the ice. Cracked it, anyway. "Come and have a beer," one of the men said. "Doug's not here, I'm his brother. What brings you to Kenora?"

Barney was wrong; they weren't all Bernier supporters. On the other hand, when a beleaguered town like Kenora has a cabinet minister representing it at Queen's Park you need a mighty good reason to oppose him, and a damned attractive alternative and these men had neither. Some of them were actively campaigning for him; others were merely voting for him. After the social amenities were dispensed with they talked and I mostly listened. They wanted to know what Doug Johnson had done to get his name in the Toronto papers and I gave the clipping to one of them; it was an hour and a half before I got it back. Meanwhile it was Bernier, Indians, the fallacy of mercury poisoning and the injustice of life and business so far from the south.

There was another group of younger people nearby — not denim generation exactly but clearly not establishment members either, and soon I was talking with them as well as the boosters. They were social workers and they, too, were defensive at first although friendlier. They wanted to tell me about their work, their view of Kenora, their mistrust of Toronto writers and eventually I moved over to their table and it was a funny thing: I didn't drink a great deal that night but I was never without a fresh glass of beer. The boosters included me in their rounds long after I'd left their table.

By now it was about nine o'clock and the social workers were beginning to think about going to work the next day. I mentioned the name of a bar where, I'd heard, the Indians tended to do their drinking (there were a few in the Kenricia, very quiet and not indulging in anything remotely akin to serious boozing); the social workers brightened up and said "Yeah, let's take the writer to the circus." I've forgotten the name of the place but it was packed with whites and Indians and very noisy. We found a table in the center of the room and I looked about. Lots of Indians, lots of whites, lots of beer and lots of noise. "Where," I asked with a straight face, "are all the drunken Indians? When are they going to start killing each other?" I was grateful for their almost apologetic laughter. "This is about as bad as it gets," one of them said.

We left after a while, adjourning to a Chinese restaurant for eggrolls and coffee and when we left the restaurant we did see a small incident. A middle-aged woman was sprawled on the sidewalk, leaning against a storefront and a policeman was holding his handkerchief over a wound on her leg. Her man had cut her and he was standing there too, looking sorrowful and befuddled.

We parted company and I was asleep by midnight.

Next morning I went to Doug Johnson's frozen food store and introduced myself (his brother apparently hadn't forewarned him, which surprised me; Kenora's a very tight little community with a highly efficient telegraph system) and at first he seemed unenthusiastic, but later I put it down to business — he knew I was going to kill his morning if not the entire day and his desk was badly cluttered. We left, inevitably, for the nearest coffee shop. Kenora's business and political affairs seem to depend on a permanent floating coffee break. The locale can be any of two or three restaurants; the faces change but the coffee break is always in progress and, as happens at the fountain of Rome, if you sit at the booth or table long enough you'll see everyone sooner or later. It's quite fascinating to watch it in action. I've noticed the same phenomenon in other towns but seldom as such an integral part of the social fabric. Probably more information is exchanged there than in the local newspaper, probably more business transacted there than in offices or town council meetings.

We sat at a booth and I removed my tape recorder and put it on the table, off to one side; coffee arrived and I asked him to tell me about Kenora, about separatism in French Canada, about anything he thought might or should interest me. He began by saying that separation isn't a burning issue in Kenora. "Most people don't perceive it as something that can actually happen. They perceive it more like western separatism. The real plank the [provincial] Progressive Conservative Party is running on is national unity. The battle between Trudeau and Lévesque will be our civil war, only we'll fight it with words and not with bullets, just as Canadians always have."

He went on to explain that people in Kenora are oriented to Manitoba, not Ontario and that rightly or wrongly (he thinks wrongly) the people think Queen's Park is interested only in southern Ontario and doesn't give a hoot for the north. "Politics," he once told a reporter, "are more important in the north than they are in the south. City councils in the south are strong, influential, more important than the member of parliament. Up here it's different." By road Toronto is nearly 1,200 miles, while Winnipeg is about 125 miles and the

Manitoba border about 40 miles, and probably Kenora would be better off as part of Manitoba than Ontario. At least, says Johnson, until Leo Bernier came along. "For years this riding was Liberal and we received nothing. It's not the same now . . . but Queen's Park must realize that we, and everyone else west of the Lakehead, are dealing mostly with Manitoba."

Nor is it Queen's Park that bothers Johnson. "It's those whiz kids," he told the reporter, "those instant experts they send in here to cure our problems. Take that plan for timber-cutting rights to Reed Paper Ltd. It would have provided a couple of thousand jobs for those who want to work. It would have been block cutting, that is, cut in such a way that it would have enhanced the wildlife.

"Yet those environmentalists in Toronto, who have never seen a forest, and couldn't even find this one, created the impression that it would have turned into a moonscape. That's not what would happen at all."

Johnson is a strong supporter of Bernier, he told me, "as is most of the town. Up here the gut issues have to do with the province and the phenomenal costs here. To sink a basement costs $5,000 of blasting. You can dig in Thunder Bay but you can't dig here. The town of Keewatin (a community of 2,000 just west of Kenora) has no sewage or water; it's just going in now and there's no way if the government weren't paying 95 per cent of it. Parts of Kenora are still unserviced, too."

He has high hopes for Bernier's new Ministry of Northern Affairs, and the $100,000,000 the province has set aside for northern Ontario priorities, "things that don't come under normal subsidizing."

Leo Bernier has created a lot of bitterness among the Indians and, to some extent, among the press but his constituents — and even his opponent in the summer election — see him as their man, a politician with clout and now with a lot of money to spend in the north. I interviewed him once in his Queen's Park office when I was writing about Grassy Narrows and the mercury pollution, and I got nowhere with him. But I was impressed with Doug Johnson and have to admit to his logic, pragmatic or not.

Johnson had some intelligent things to say about the Indians, too. "It isn't Minamata disease," he told me, "it's that they've got no economic base. We've got to create some dignity for these people and there are a number of ways we could do this. First the commercial fishing has to be revived; so let the Indians fish the waterways out. Whitefish aren't carnivores, the pickerel are OK up to 16 inches and we aren't putting any more mercury in there." In other words, hire the Indians to fish the waterway clean, bury the contaminated fish or turn them into fertilizer. Maybe do some dredging. Then restock with healthy fish.

"Reopen the fishing lodges," he says. "Lease them to the Indians for a dollar a year and let people catch not just six pickerel but a hundred."

And he added, somewhat caustically, that "a lot of Kenora people say they wouldn't live anywhere else [which is understandable; it's magnificent country to live in, and an attractive town, too]. It would be interesting to see, if the town mill closed down, how many people would actually leave the town. Ontario-Minnesota Pulp and Paper employs 800 people. If they were suddenly out of jobs, and there were plenty in Thunder Bay, how many of them would go to Thunder Bay and how many would go on welfare? So you can't entirely blame the Indians."

Barney Lamm has concocted a similar scheme for the lodges. He'd reopen them, including his own, on the government's much-ridiculed "fish for fun" basis, letting guests catch as many fish as they could on the polluted waterways, burying them, and a couple of days a week flying them to lakes where they could catch and eat unpolluted fish. It would require government subsidizing but, he reasons, what you lose on the subsidy you'd make up on the welfare. The Grassy Narrows Indians used very little welfare until the fishing lodges closed down. They don't have the welfare tradition, not yet.

Speak of the devil, he's sure to appear. Barney wandered in and joined us, and when he and Doug Johnson began covering the same ground I excused myself to check out of the Kenricia Hotel; my bus would leave about seven o'clock that evening.

Having put my bags in a locker at the bus depot, I checked the schedule and returned to the restaurant where they were still talking. Barney said he wanted to go and have a look at Ball Lake Lodge; would I like to come along for the ride?

"Will you get me back by seven o'clock?" I asked, and he assured me he would. We left about twenty minutes later in a float-equipped Otter with a third man, now a government worker, who, when in his teens had worked for Barney at the lodge as a guide. It's about a half hour's flight and I spent the time gazing down at the countryside, perhaps 2,500 feet below ruminating on the cruel pranks that have been inflicted on what we now call Canada, by glaciers and ocean currents, which stripped away the soil (exposing the minerals, to be sure) and which created such a harsh and unforgiving land. We were flying over the stark beauty of the boreal forest; its thin, acid soil won't grow much but pine trees which cling to the rock, roots desperately probing tiny crevices for nourishment. Here and there were ruins of cabins and shacks where trappers, miners and bankrupted tourist lodge operators tried and failed to settle and live. At this same latitude in Europe, roughly between London and Paris, they can grow palm trees and wine grapes and the climate is soft and the land lush. Here the land we claim but cannot seem to develop stretches perhaps two thousand miles further north — much more if you include the Arctic islands — and today even the Indians, who have lived here for thousands of years, can no longer make a go of it. It seemed to me both exciting country and desolate, as empty as Diefenbaker's great Northern Vision; a vast and mighty nation when viewed on a classroom globe, fragile and overwhelming when viewed from 2,500 feet. When we touched down at Barney's lodge, a group of Indians and the white couple he employs to keep watch over the place waded into the water to wrestle the float plane to shore. The quiet after the drone of the aircraft engine was heavy and we didn't talk much for there was nothing to say; the deserted cabins and lodge said it all. The sand beach and the paths were slick with caterpillars which had stripped the leaves from poplar stands and birch trees. The birch, at least would survive; they had sprouted tiny new leaves which would see them through the season but it was eerie, more like late autumn than early summer.

Barney took us on a tour of the place as he had several years before, ostensibly to check on the condition of the buildings but in fact, I think, to quietly grieve the loss of a life he had loved.

There are popcorn machines in one of the boathouses on the main dock which I'd asked about on my last visit and Barney had chuckled. When the tourists came in from a day's fishing, the staff would tie their boats up, take away their fishing tackle to wash down, leaving them empty-handed as they ascended to the main dock. "The only thing you have to carry here is your wallet," Barney used to tell his guests, "and we'll even lighten that for you." As they passed the popcorn booth free bags of popcorn were handed to the tourists, which they'd munch on as they walked to their cabins; of course the popcorn was heavily salted and invariably they'd decide to head first for the bar in the main lodge. Somehow they suddenly felt very thirsty.

The money came in. Barney Lamm freely admits the place was a goldmine for twenty years. But much of the money went to the Indians he employed, and it occurred to me that money earned tends to be spent on food and clothing and snowmobile parts, while money doled out in welfare cheques invariably gets spent in Kenora's bars.

We drank tea with the couple who care for the place, chatted with the Indians who come in to do basic maintenance, and flew back to Kenora several hours later, accompanied by some of the Indians who piled into the back of the plane to spend the weekend in town. I was feeling somewhat subdued and I guess Barney was, too. A normally gregarious man who loves to talk, he piloted the plane silently, an unlit cigar clamped firmly in his mouth. We made desultory attempts at joviality as we parted company on the aircraft dock and then I left, climbing the hill toward the bus depot.

The bus was almost ready. I made sure that my suitcase was aboard and stood, smoking while I waited and then an Indian came by, lurching a little, peering into the group of passengers. He saw me and approached, talking, but his speech was so slurred by alcohol I couldn't understand much of what he was saying. He told me his name and accepted a cigarette and it came to me that he was trying to tell me something important; there was a sense of frustrated urgency about him. It was important, but he had forgotten what it was. I handed him a two dollar bill and he studied it for a long moment and said, very slowly, "You're giving me money."

"I thought maybe you could use it," I said rather lamely.

"I'm not bad off for money right now," he intoned.

"If you don't need it you can give it back," I said. I was perplexed. He studied the bill a moment, pocketed it and started trying to remember what it was he had wanted to say and he followed me onto the bus. I nodded to tell the driver not to interfere and he kept telling me there was something he had to tell me. Finally he looked me in the eye, then glanced at my bulging pocket and in conspiratorial whisper asked "Are we on tape?"

And suddenly I understood. I lifted the flap of the pocket and showed him the small tape recorder, and whispered back, as conspiratorially as I could, "Don't worry, I got every word."

He breathed a sigh of relief, patted my shoulder and left the bus with the help of the driver. He passed by my window and waved briefly, then walked unsteadily off. His mission had been accomplished even if he had forgotten what it was. There were tears in my eyes as I put it all together. I'd spent a week at Grassy Narrows once and I'd been seen interviewing people. The word had spread; he and I had probably met and talked before and he'd remembered that much. Now I knew what he'd come to tell me, what it was so urgent to say. It was "help".

THE BUS ROLLED into Thunder Bay about midnight for a thirty-minute "lunch" break. I collected my suitcase and called a cab telling the driver to "take me to the nearest, nicest hotel in town."

He started driving but shook his head saying "Gee, I don't know, Mac . . ." When he called his dispatcher, she said

"There's a Lions' convention going on and there isn't a room in town." We barely made it back to the bus. I climbed wearily on board again, hoisted my bags to the overhead rack and pulled out the map, worn and grimy and barely legible by now, wondering where I could find a bed. I knew instinctively that I was in for a long, long ride, and was frustrated because I knew what to expect, what it would cost me and I was ill-prepared. Exhaustion. I've never been able to sleep on a bus; I'm too long and the seats don't go back far enough. Communities along the north shore of Lake Superior are small and motel operators are difficult to rouse at three or four o'clock in the morning so I sat on that bus for twenty hours, all the way from Kenora to Sault Ste. Marie, more than 750 miles. I guess I must have anticipated that something like this would happen, for I'd bought six cans of beer before leaving Kenora, something I hadn't done before. And that is how I became involved with a young man who writes poetry about "the amnesty of my dreams", a man who had just gotten out of prison in British Columbia after serving three years for grand larceny and a 23-year-old waiter/artist from Montreal. He was French and had been raised in Montreal and New Brunswick. While visiting British Columbia, he'd found an art school in Victoria that he wanted to attend and now he was heading for Toronto, to raise a stake of $3,000 or $4,000 by working in a restaurant to finance it. He was pretty contemptuous of René Lévesque and told me Quebec would never secede. I asked him how he could be so certain of that: "René Lévesque is in power," he reasoned, "and he wants to stay in power and increase the power and the French culture. There's no way he's going to separate. If they held the referendum now it would fail, so there won't be a referendum."

I wasn't in any mood to argue and let it go, although I hope there aren't many people taking such a simplistic view. He told me he'd been existing on $72 Unemployment Insurance cheques and he'd spent his last $99 on bus fare from Victoria to Toronto. He'd been on the bus for four and a half days straight and all he really wanted was a shower.

We opened my six-pack and an Australian woman across

the aisle joined in, her husband asleep beside her, and told me that he was an education administrator and had three months' leave. They were doing the whole continent, San Francisco to New York City, then Europe and home and she was astonished at the Quebec situation and wondered where it would end. Her husband woke up briefly and drowsily reached into his bag for a bottle of Coppertone, which he carefully and liberally smeared on his face, then went immediately back to sleep. They'd been on the road six weeks, she said, non-stop. We talked for a while before the Australian woman went to sleep and then the French Canadian beside me, and I lulled myself into the stupor that substitutes for sleep as we sped through the night. We had a twenty minute breakfast stop somewhere, arriving in Sault Ste. Marie in the early afternoon and I checked into the Windsor Hotel. Of course I couldn't sleep, I was beyond it, so I walked the streets, in zombie fashion, for about an hour and a half, returned to the hotel and typed some notes and eventually went to bed. I'd been on the road for nineteen days and I was barely half way across Canada. I wondered if I would survive. I spent two nights there, mostly sleeping or typing, trying to recall the people, the conversations, the countryside, trying to make some sense out of it all and finding it impossible.

What I was getting was fragments of people's lives, uninformed and apathetic opinions about Quebec, about Canada; no one really seemed to care very much about anything beyond their own affairs, and the prospect of a hot shower or a decent breakfast or the chance of a job a thousand miles away transcended problems of national unity. It was exasperating and I recalled a quotation I once heard attributed to Sir John A. Macdonald: "I would be quite willing, personally, to leave the whole country a wilderness for the next half-century but I fear that if Englishmen do not go there [i.e. settle the far west] Yankees will."

Well, we've managed to leave most of the country a wilderness for more than a century; as for the Yankees, they own us and except for a handful of nationalist academics, politicians and journalists, nobody seems to care. When I traveled through the United States I found people polarized and deeply committed; bigoted, some of them, stubborn and often foolish, but seldom apathetic: they were *Americans,* and anyone who disagreed was *the enemy* and be damned to them. They held positive opinions on practically anything which they'd share for the asking. Here in my own country I was finding people aimless, out of touch with each other and uninterested: drifting, divided, curiously confident that life will continue and little will change. There were exceptions, of course, but the mass of opinion lacked consensus. Unfathomable and, I think, appalling. More and more I found myself thinking not about how to keep the country together but what it will be like — how chaotic, how poverty-stricken — if the nation is carved into slices. I began accepting, reluctantly, the possibility, rejecting René Lévesque as villain or cause or anything but catalyst: being Canadian just doesn't seem to mean much anymore. Not on the buses I traveled on, at least.

Thus it was refreshing to meet Ed Deibel in North Bay the following day, a man I'd heard wanted to declare northern Ontario a country and whom I'd mentally written off as a crackpot, an eccentric who might be worth a giggle and little more. When I telephoned him, we arranged to meet at my hotel and when I asked how I'd recognize him he burst out laughing. "Don't worry about that," he said. "You'll know who I am."

Well, he was right about that and I was dead wrong about him. He wandered into the hotel lobby wearing loud, green-checked trousers, a ridiculous flowered shirt left open to display a sweatshirt with a large red zig zag maple leaf he'd filched from our flag and the letters N.O.H.P. emblazoned over it, standing for Northern Ontario Heritage Party. He's a paunchy man of 44 and he was carrying two enormous ring-bound files, each about eight inches thick and containing 10,600 signatures of people supporting his cause. He was toting scrapbooks and looseleaf files as well, these chronicling his adventures over the past four years.

"I'm a self-educated person," he told me. "I worked for the Bell Telephone from 1952 to 1962. I started as a janitor and then got into installation and cable repairs. I learn quick; it was a class one job. Then I got into pressurization of cables. I built the Arizona Motel on the outskirts of town while I was with the Bell. It took me twenty-two months, working in my spare time. It had sixteen units and a 40-site trailer park and I waited five years to sell it and did very well out of it and now I'm taking a year off."

We were sitting in my hotel room, the only quiet place I could find, with the tape recorder on; mostly I just listened, and the longer I listened the more impressed I became. His self-education didn't concentrate too heavily on English, his grammar and syntax need a lot of work, which probably costs him points in the hallowed offices of Queen's Park, but his logic seems flawless and I suspect he'll cause a good deal of political mischief before he's through. That would likely be a very good thing for northern Ontario and probably southern Ontario too, although what he wants, primarily, is to separate the two, creating an eleventh province. Draw a line from Parry Sound to Ottawa, give Deibel's party everything north of the line, and he'll use the resources — pulp and paper and minerals — to blackmail Queen's Park into industrializing the north. Best to tell it in his own words, paraphrased and rearranged because we covered a lot of ground in the next hour and a half.

"It began in April, 1973, when the Ontario budget came out and they were going to have a seven per cent tax on heat and light, and I said there was no way I was going to pay; I'd go to jail first. The local media were notified and the next day the phone started ringing. We had a meeting of about 500 people, formed a Tax Repeal Committee in two weeks, and within five weeks we had 24,000 signatures from all over the north. Eventually the tax was removed. There were a lot of people who simply wanted it cut back to five per cent but there was a third group that wanted a new province. So on May 16, 1973, I said I was going to find out how much support there was in the north for this and I formed the New Province Committee. I got 600 members and got a petition of 6,000 signatures which we presented to Premier Davis in the fall of 1974. I camped on the lawn in front of Queen's Park for three days with this petition, to ask the premier if he'd give northerners a vote on the question of a new province, and of course he said no. I had a twenty-minute interview with him.

"So I came home and we asked ourselves two questions. One, should 50 per cent of our natural resources be processed and manufactured to finished product right here in northern Ontario? Two, should we do our part to preserve prime agricultural land in southern Ontario for growing food? In other words have the industrial expansion move north. We have a tremendous amount of wealth here, in minerals and forest products, but it's all shipped south."

It was when the oldest of his three sons found he couldn't get a job in northern Ontario that Deibel began to get aroused, and soon he learned that since 1961 more than 140,000 young people have been forced to leave the north. Improvement of educational facilities has worsened the problem. "There seems to be a feeling at Queen's Park that we're just moose pasture and Christmas trees, miners and chainsaw operators."

Deibel and his supporters approached the commissioner of elections to find out what they had to do to form a new political party and were told they needed 10,000 signatures — not members, just signatures. And they couldn't incorporate the word "independent" in the name of their party.

"We started the blitz on September 17, 1976, quit on November 1, lapsed for the winter and started again in the spring; when they called the election we had our 10,000 signatures. We've got about 10,600 now, from 144 northern communities and 17 southern Ontario communities — we got about 500 from them."

That didn't mean they were ready to fight an election, but they have the political framework they need for the next one. I asked Deibel what the main thrust of his campaign would be and he explained, not angrily but almost pedantically: a tourist motel operator's lecture to a class of one, in politics and economics.

"We've been neglected, mismanaged and exploited," he told me, "and we're not going to accept being treated like a colony. We aren't going to continue to let them extract the wealth of the north. We want the Ontario Mining Act enforced, and the act prohibits exporting raw material to a foreign country, states that it must be processed in Canada. This act is being blatantly misused. Falconbridge ships their ore to Norway to be processed. We have no zinc smelter. Six million tons of iron ore pellets leave Thunder Bay to go to the United States and there should be a steel smelter there, in the Thunder Bay area.

"We believe — and we've got the research to know this — that if you want to create wealth out of raw materials, by the time they're processed to finished product they've increased in value one hundred times. In the past three years they've taken out $7.2 billion in raw materials and you don't have to be a mathematician to figure out that if you processed them you'd be talking about $720 billion. The figures are staggering. In 1974 you could take $60 worth of iron ore and build a Cadillac worth $10,000. And a lot of the land is useless for anything else. We could put manufacturing plants on rock piles that are no good for anything else. We figure that $2.5 billion worth of raw materials leave northern Ontario annually.

"We don't want to separate but there's nothing in the British North America Act that says you can't create a new province. We started out with four and we've got ten today and an eleventh province wouldn't be separate — we'd have the same powers as the others. There are 805,000 people living in northern Ontario and there should be three or four million. We're one of the richest countries in the world but it's all potential. What we want to do is achieve it. We need the policies to do so. We can become the industrial heart of Canada. We're sixty miles west of The Sault — this is the center of Canada. We have 80 per cent of the province in land mass, 95 per cent of the natural resources, and less than ten per cent of the population. We have 20 billion tons of iron ore reserves. We have copper, zinc, uranium, silver, platinum, gold, nickel, hell there are 19 precious metals and we have 15 of them.

"Reed Paper produces only rough pulp. If the pulp and paper industry were to produce a finished product you could create 200,000 jobs in northern Ontario.

"There are three political parties in Ontario and they just

aren't giving us good government in the north and we're not going to accept this anymore — that's what these ten thousand signatures mean. Unemployment in North Bay is about 5,000 but if you go north it increases to 17 per cent in the smaller communities. That's really heavy unemployment.

"There are two problems. One is that 85 per cent of our extraction industries are foreign-owned and they want to keep their own industries going. The other is the transportation policy, if there is such a thing. We can ship raw materials very cheaply. As raw material is processed and refined the rate increases, which means you can ship raw material away, have it processed and manufactured somewhere else and when the product comes back to the consumer the rate is ten times as high."

Quebec, Deibel said, has given the north a shot in the arm. "There was a feeling of hopelessness for a long time, that there was nothing we could do. What Quebec has done is show a lot of people there *is* something you can do. I don't believe in what he's [Lévesque] done and I don't think Quebec will separate but the response here has been that you *can* do something."

Deibel isn't exactly worried about Quebec and certainly he empathizes with René Lévesque. "I don't trust Trudeau," he told me, "because when I hear remarks made by a minister like Marc Lalonde that if Quebec separates, his allegiance is to Quebec, then I don't know how that minister can serve Canadians. And Trudeau has said that if Quebec separates he would go to live in Quebec. He's got to prove to me that he's a *Canadian* because I think a crucial point in Canadian history is that Quebeckers are Canadians *first*. Is Trudeau a Canadian or a Quebecker? I think he's more of a Quebecker. I feel that René Lévesque is economic and I agree with a lot of his economic solutions. You have got to be able to control the economy from within the provinces. The asbestos, for instance, that it has to be processed within Quebec. On language I think he's way out of line, he's suppressing English Canadians in Quebec . . ."

Deibel's no crackpot. If his political dreams come true he'd have a province with a population greater than Newfoundland, Prince Edward Island and New Brunswick, and roughly equal to Nova Scotia, Manitoba and Saskatchewan. "We're reasonable men," he once said, "but it's the only alternative left."

Meanwhile in southern Ontario's Golden Horseshoe around the western end of Lake Ontario we're paving and industrializing the best agricultural land in Canada as fast as we can because the land is worth far more as factory sites than farms and orchards. But there's a Midas touch to that kind of development. What are we going to do for food? Eat pine cones and iron ore pellets? With the Great Lakes and good rail connections at the Lakehead, industrializing the north makes a lot of sense, and if it takes political blackmail to achieve it, then let it be so. And while many English Canadians, and not a few French Canadians, are angry with Lévesque, he's nonetheless feeding the hopes of the have-nots, providing a feast of precedent. Hell, he could wind up as one of Canada's greatest statesmen, a national hero. It's a mind-blowing thought, isn't it?

And as for controlling the economy from within the provinces, it may sound simplistic and naive, but who better? At least they *care* about their futures, and it seems inconceivable to me that they could do any worse than Ottawa and Washington have done.

And certainly Deibel's right about southern attitudes toward the north. We're very comfortable down here and, like the Americans, we want to keep our own industries going, keep our own jobs. If that means exploiting other parts of Canada then, politically at least, we have the clout to do it: traditionally, *historically,* we have steadily demonstrated our willingness, our intention to continue doing it. The political reality may have changed, our clout may be only an illusion we have been able to maintain up to now. If northerners and westerners won't buy it anymore then let them grab what they can. I'd be delighted to see the ruralization of southern Ontario.

NEXT MORNING I embarked on the nine-hour, 360-mile run that would take me out of Ontario and deposit me in Montreal.

It was a fairly uneventful day and I found myself reflecting on a curious fact.

It was now only a couple of days before Ontario's ill-fated election (and Premier William Davis' well-deserved rebuff) and I'd heard practically nothing about it. Sometimes I think you can find out more about what's on people's minds by paying attention to what they aren't talking about, and what they weren't talking about in northern Ontario was Bill Davis. If I tried to raise the subject I would often sense an embarrassment that his supporters felt for him, and a passive resentment over a contrived and needless election.

It was a complicated political equation but my reading of it was that Davis, ill-advised, was persuaded to seek majority government. He attempted to make national unity his main talking point, perhaps in a bid to increase his national stature, but all that the people were interested in was unemployment. Few people knew the political basis for calling an election — a minor and uncontroversial opposition amendment to rent control that the Government itself was uninterested in. Perhaps Davis was lured by the polls, which showed he had made a dramatic leap in personal popularity; perhaps he felt he could take advantage of what he perceived as weak leadership of the opposition parties. Perhaps he was just plain greedy. At least two of his own backbenchers had warned that polls they had taken in their own ridings indicated a strong majority of their constituents were opposed to an election. The last one had been held just nineteen months before, and anyway minority government had been working well. It had "cleared away the accumulated cobwebs of thirty-two years of rule by one party. It brought a new spark and zing to the proceedings in the lofty, ornate legislature."

That was the *Toronto Star*'s Jonathan Manthorpe, writing shortly after the election had been called, and he continued: "William Davis, surprisingly, perhaps, took to minority government with relish. He quickly put the horror of near defeat behind him and plunged into the new reality. The image he had carried around since 1971 of a man whose only interest was power faded, and it became clear that here was a someone who really loved politics . . . . Minority government produced moderation. It produced moderation in legislation. It produced moderation in debate. It produced clear and temperate thought.''

I thought it a good column, and I was both frustrated and relieved by the fact that I would be on the road and unable to vote. I hoped Davis would get exactly what he got, and that he would respond to it with grace and get back to the business of running the province. If I'd been home I'd have been in a dilemma: how do you rap a politician's knuckles without risking a reversal? Even after thirty-four years of Tory rule — and some of those years were turbulent with scandal and ineptitude — I wasn't yet prepared for either of the opposition parties to take over simply because I didn't think *they* were ready. Basically I'm conservative, not Conservative; I've voted in all directions. I suppose I'd have either stayed home or arranged, if possible, a deal with my wife to cancel each other's ballots. Neither is satisfying.

Ontario has its own French-English problems, complicated by the diverse ethnic population of Toronto, and we've been experiencing some ugly backlash and bigotry. So be it. There are people in the province of Ontario who dislike French Canadians. As a weekly commuter to Quebec for two years I know there are people there who despise English Canadians. That is regrettable but relatively unimportant. But while I believe that Quebeckers will determine their own destiny, I'm damned if I'll let them pretend that the Government of Ontario is unconcerned, or that it will tolerate what bigotries may exist. Thus what occurred in Essex County and in Cavan Township bears examination, as does the Government's response to both cases.

One of the essential duties of a democracy is, as I see it, to protect the rights of its minorities, and the 90,000 citizens of Ontario who speak only French are indeed a particularly significant minority. Our treatment of them is an unmistakable symbol to Quebec of our national intentions. René Lévesque may not give us any medals for behaving decently, but we needn't give him the bullets to shoot us with.

For eight long years the 50,000 French-speaking residents

of Essex County, in the Chatham area, had been trying to get French language instruction and for eight long years the Essex County board of education had balked. As feelings intensified, the French community hardened its attitude and demanded not just instruction but the building of a French language high school. On March 8, 1976, the matter came to a vote and was defeated, twelve to five.

Ontario's education minister, Tom Wells, had warned that if the Essex board wouldn't build the school he'd pass legislation forcing them to do so, and he went so far as to raise the provincial government's share of the estimated $4.8 million the school would cost from 77 per cent to 95.5 per cent, meaning the cost to Essex would be cut from $117,000 to a paltry $24,000.

The first white settlers in the area were French, Wells pointed out, "yet they were deprived of this one thing which they see as a symbol of their heritage and their culture." He immediately prepared the necessary legislation and it was stalled on the order paper by the election. As soon as the election was over, the bill was passed by the Legislature, supported by both Opposition Leader Stephen Lewis and Liberal Leader Stuart Smith (although their local candidates broke ranks and opposed it during the campaign).

Lewis later said the bill "reaffirms the intention of the Ontario Legislature to say to Essex County, the province, Quebec and Canada that Francophone rights, language and culture are sacrosanct as an indispensable component of this country."

Wells, when he originally introduced the bill observed quite rightly that he was not interfering with local autonomy. "This matter has gone well past the issue of local autonomy," he said. "It is a provincial and national issue."

There are twenty-four such schools operating in the province and the law now stipulates that minority language instruction must be provided wherever French population warrants it. Thus the matter was resolved, late perhaps, but nonetheless.

In the fall there was another ugly little situation developing.

Cavan Township Council, in the Cobourg area, turned down a rezoning application which would have enabled a group of six bilingual Cistercian monks to establish a monastery within the township. They had chosen a farm where they would continue making cheese, as they had been doing at Oka, in Quebec.

Cavan township council made no bones about the reason for turning down the application. Councillor Joe Thompson said that "it's a Protestant township and it shall stay like this." Cavan township farmer Melville Morrison put it more bluntly: "Maybe I'm bigoted, but Catholics and French are a bad mixture. French Catholics are the worst kind there is."

Tough and insulting language but not very important. There are similar attitudes in Quebec, directed at English non-Catholics. The important thing to me was Attorney General Roy McMurtry's immediate response. He found it regrettable, he said, involving serious discrimination that might require special legislation. That from a Protestant representing one of Toronto's most notorious WASP ridings.

McMurtry had just emerged from another controversy, over his refusal to allow Montreal businessman Gerard Filion a French language trial. Filion, former publisher of *Le Devoir*, is one of 19 people charged with conspiracy to rig dredging contract prices, and McMurtry said that since the charge was one of conspiracy, Filion's case could not be separated from the others. Instead he offered simultaneous translation services throughout the trial.

McMurtry's resulting unpopularity in Quebec was an irony. More than a year before, recognizing the high proportion of French-speaking people in the Sudbury region, he announced that trials in French would be made available. He also mentioned that French language courts in Sudbury, Ottawa and l'Orignal served more than 47,000 people — more than half of Ontario's unilingual French population. And he said that extension of such services in Kapuskasing, Cochrane and Hornepayne would raise the figure to sixty-six per cent of the 90,000 total unilingual population. "I guess I feel a little funny about it," he told *Star* writer Charlotte Montgomery. "I feel, with due modesty, that we have accomplished a lot. I find it a gentle irony — having been the first attorney general in this province to tackle this matter — that I would be the one to bear the brunt of the Filion case."

He was able to take some comfort, he said, from a letter written by Senator Eugene Forsey, pointing out that while Ontario has been slow it should not be criticized for not having a bilingual legal system comparable to that developed in Quebec over the period of a century. At the time of Confederation the French-speaking population was so small in Ontario that the province "never even thought of official bilingualism . . . there is not the faintest hint of it in any of the Confederation documents."

In fact, Section 133 of the British North America Act states:

"Either the English or the French Language may be used by any Person in the Debates of the Houses of Parliament of Canada and of the Houses of the Legislature of Quebec; and both those Languages shall be used in the respective Records and Journals of those Houses; and either of those Languages may be used by any Person or in any Pleading or Process in or issuing from any Court of Canada established under this Act, and in or from all or any of the Courts of Quebec.

"The Acts of the Parliament of Canada and of the Legislature of Quebec shall be printed and published in both those Languages."

Nevertheless, it has become a political reality that the spirit rather than the letter of the British North America Act be followed. Thus McMurtry has begun an expanding program of providing French language services in the courts of *Ontario* [the Act stipulates only federal courts]; there are an inadequate but growing number of French language educational facilities; there is French television and radio. Above all, there is a growing acceptance and encouragement from Queen's Park for the rights of French-speaking people living in Ontario. That is a good deal more than can be said for the attitude of the Lévesque government, which is still a Canadian provincial government, with its own minorities to care for.

Premier Davis does appear to be most reluctant to make any move toward making French an official language in Ontario, however, and he has been subjected to some criticism for this. Presumably the main reason for this lack of enthusiasm would be his belief that the people of Ontario don't want to go that far and he may well be correct about that. Certainly Toronto is a cosmopolitan city. Ten per cent of the city's people are Italian, the rest are a mixture of just about everything and there are foreign language classes in some downtown schools. Many ethnics cannot sympathize with French Canadian aspirations at all.

But if Davis is politically correct — and I'm not entirely convinced of that — he is nonetheless missing an important opportunity to weaken the arguments of separatists in Quebec. If Ontario were to adopt French as an official language it would be an unmistakable gesture going far beyond mere tokens of commitment to Confederation.

I did not travel through south central Ontario on my journey because that is where I live. I felt that it would be more useful to travel the northern route, taking samples at home on my return, and two people I talked with after the trip gave me unorthodox and surprising comments.

One of these was Fern Beaudoin, a 35-year-old, self-employed contractor who lives with his wife and daughter in Ajax, a half hour's drive from Toronto. He has worked in Ontario since he was a teenager and it's paid off handsomely: he owns his home, he's not wealthy but he's never unemployed and in his spare time he's building a two-seater amphibious airplane in his basement. He expects it will take him about four years, and will cost about $5,000. Fern has fifteen brothers and sisters, most of them living in the Geraldton-Long Lac area north of Lake Superior, and he plans to set up a trailer there one day, beside a lake. He'll fly there when it pleases him, to do some fishing, using the trailer as a cottage. It's the North American dream and variations of it come true frequently here for countless men like him, who come from Europe or Asia or Australia or even, like him, from Quebec.

"I don't feel French Canadian," he told me.

"Pragmatic?" I asked.

"Yeah," he said, "I go with the wind."

"What will you do if Quebec secedes?"

"Just carry on the way I'm doing now."

His wife, Hélène, is northern Ontario French; they met in Geraldton. He speaks to her in French, she answers in English and their daughter speaks only English. None of the three are trying to prove anything; it's just that he speaks more easily in French and his wife finds it natural to speak English.

They tried to encourage their daughter to speak French once, by sending her to visit family in Sherbrooke, but she discovered an American family in the house next door with a daughter her age and that was the end of that. It happens all the time in Ontario. We call it assimilation.

I also spent an evening with a neighbor who is Dutch, married to a woman from South Africa. They have two children, both of them enrolled in one of Toronto's five public school experiments with total French language immersion. Both children, 12 and seven years old, are fluent now, taking half their classes in English and half in French. Their father speaks English and French as well as his native Dutch and their mother, who moved from England to South Africa when she was ten years old, speaks some Afrikaans and some French.

Here, then, are two Canadian immigrants who have chosen to raise bilingual children with no interest in teaching them to speak Dutch and I asked why. "First of all," he told me, "it's a bilingual country; and secondly, with English and French you can get around most of the world. Also, French is a very good base for the Latin languages. We could only see advantages, we couldn't see disadvantages."

Clear enough. But when I asked him what he thought of the Lévesque election and subsequent events he told me, "I don't think it has done the case of bilingualism and biculturalism any good. It has polarized the situation and I would think there will be some backlash here, a declining interest in French programs, although I can't prove that . . . . Personally, I still feel very strongly that to have one nation you should have one language, one official language. Now whether that should be French or

English is debatable. When you think of all the complaints about American influence, maybe it would be better to have a unilingual French Canada. That will, of course, never happen but it's an interesting possibility. If you want to make Canada different from the United States, a different culture, that's the way to do it."

But how could he square the decision to have the children educated in French, with the distinct possibility that they might suffer in other subjects because of a language gap? "Well," he said, "I consider French to be one of the major world languages, English, French and Spanish."

So it wasn't a case of Canadian patriotism but recognition of the value of French. I had pointed out to him that many new Canadians have been depicted as hostile to French Canadian aspirations and he contradicted me.

"A large majority of the children (who attend the immersion classes) are of immigrant parents. Generally we find that immigrants have more sense of adventure about the whole thing than second or third generation Canadians, I don't know why. I suppose they came into the country with another language — in Europe the influence of French is much stronger — so they feel more at ease coping in a bilingual situation. . . ."

He didn't believe Lévesque's referendum would go through. "I think that the Québécois will, by and large, be fairly pragmatic about the whole thing. They'll look at the economic effects of separation and . . . very likely vote against it."

By MID-AFTERNOON the bus was passing through Ottawa, which gave me a perverse pleasure. The nation's capital strikes me as a totally subjective city for anyone who doesn't live there, almost a frame of mind. I had toyed with the idea of stopping over for a couple of days and decided that even if I could spend a month there it would tend to confuse rather than enlighten me. I had spoken with friends there before I'd embarked on my journey and would be talking to others on my return and I've sat in enough cabinet ministers', mandarins' and opposition members' waiting rooms over the years to be highly skeptical about the chance of gaining much information, any insights into current Canadian reality.

My version of Ottawa is a contrived city filled with people who are so involved in the game of politics that one inevitably gets caught up in it; this can be very exciting but not necessarily illuminating. Later I would talk with the people whose judgments I trust and whose intuitions I value and would find few grounds for regret. At least no more regret than I felt in bypassing Hamilton, Chatham, or all of southern Ontario. My journey was hardly a scientific sampling of Canadian opinion — you can get that from the Gallup polls. It was more of an experiential thing which, combined with other journeys I have taken over the years, would increase my sense of nationality; there were many important centers that I would have to miss.

One of the people I talked to when the trip was ended was Doug Fisher, one-time New Democratic Member of Parliament and longtime parliamentary journalist, and he made an observation which reminded me that besides being the most totally, if somewhat hypocritical and self-consciously, bilingual city in English-speaking Canada, Ottawa is also our most spectacular evidence of bicultural and bilingual failure.

Fisher takes a dim view of so-called national unity. I had asked what he thought the people of Quebec would eventually do and he said he'd written it eleven years ago, for the United Church *Observer*: "They're gone. It may take eight or ten more years to work out, but the conception of Canada and Confederation that we've had is indefensible and can't last."

Then he went on to say that if bilingualism could ever work, "then the Parliamentary press gallery should be the perfect expression of it, but the figures are interesting. There are now approximately 220 people who are members of the gallery and of them about 45 are French Canadians, but of those 45 only 24 *work* in the French language."

He concludes from this that there is an inordinately greater interest among English-speaking Canadians than French-speaking Canadians in federal matters. And he told me that "the two groups don't mix. There's no great antagonism but there really are two isolations."

I can't accept his ultimate prognosis but neither can I reject it.

"Bilingualism is a dead issue for Canada," René Lévesque told reporters shortly after his election victory. "We don't want to shove French down anyone's throat. Bilingualism was only an attempt at keeping Quebec in Confederation. It didn't work and now it's irrelevant."

Curiously, high school students are showing less and less interest in studying French, but in Toronto universities enrollment in French courses — not just language but literature as well — is up as much as fifty per cent. I think I know why, too. I studied French through high school some years ago. My highest mark on a term examination was 97 per cent. I do not speak French because I was not *taught* to speak French; I was taught to conjugate verbs and to memorize vocabulary. I learned to do these things quite well. In the universities they teach you to listen to the sounds using the language laboratories and maybe this is filtering down to the high schools now; I hope so. I knew perfectly well in my high school years that I would consistently pass my French exams, and that I would not learn to speak French. I've been trying to ever since, sporadically, through extension courses and the like. Most recently I spent a term at the University of Toronto's School of Continuing Studies. The instructor was a woman from France and I was amused. She seemed to think we were studying French because we wanted to visit Paris, about which she reminisced incessantly. And maybe some of us did. But I was there because I feel crippled, as a Canadian journalist, without it. And because I feel awkward as just another English-speaking tourist. I'm a citizen, damn it, not a tourist.

Fisher took issue with what I suppose he thinks is a simplistic attitude on the part of people like Trudeau whose circumstances enabled them to learn both languages, and who look at the number of French Canadians who have become bilingual. If they can do it, then English Canadians can too.

"But they don't realize," he told me, "the desperate economic circumstances that forced the French Canadians to become bilingual. They think it's easy."

That cut very deep. I hadn't thought of it before, but now I must accept it: the reason I don't speak French has nothing to do with inept teaching in my high school years (although it was inept). The reason is that I don't have to speak the language: it is not an economic imperative.

THE BUS ROLLED across the Quebec border and I alternated between enjoying the shifting scenery and browsing through some newspapers I'd been collecting since Winnipeg. Their collective verdict was unanimous: there was only one issue in the Davis campaign and that was jobs. People were being bombarded with pessimistic unemployment forecasts and I was beginning to realize that until we can find some way to order our economy we may not be able to take a detached and productive attitude toward resolving the question of national unity.

That could be dangerous. Péquistes seem to think that until they jettison the rest of Canada they won't be able to achieve economic security and if they can persuade the populace of that, the referendum could squeak through.

In Ontario, and perhaps elsewhere, I think we've reached an impasse. We want to persuade Quebec, many of us, that our intentions are golden and that we're ready to talk things over, to consider a new accommodation, maybe even a new constitution. But the Péquistes have advanced beyond what they see as futile discussions. They're working among themselves to kindle a new nationalism, and they don't seem to be listening to us anymore.

QUEBEC
La Belle Bête Noire

ACROSS THE river, opposite the Parliament Buildings in Ottawa, lies Hull, the sulphurous city that is barely but fiercely Quebec. It is perhaps the most perfect expression of the national malaise.

It isn't really Hull any more, it's the Regional Community of Outaouais, with the population currently at about 100,000. Old habits, however, are difficult to break and I still think of it as Hull, an unhappy alliance between Ontario and Quebec which demonstrates much of the ugliness of the Confederation rift.

Never an attractive city, Hull has been despised and insulted over the years, and until the late 1960s, largely ignored by federal politicians, unless the wind was blowing from the wrong quarter and the fumes from the huge E. B. Eddy Co. pulp and paper plant made Hull's presence undeniable. "The Eddy plant," growled the Ottawa *Citizen*, "is an anachronism . . . it has no place in the heart of a metropolitan community."

Ottawa has long wanted to be regarded as a very metropolitan community. The people of Hull just want to survive and the 132-acre paper mill employs a large segment of the populace. It is the backbone of Hull's economy. It also smells terrible, and its position directly across the river from the Parliament Buildings makes it one of our most prominent eyesores.

In 1969 the National Capital Commission decided to relocate a large chunk of the federal bureaucracy in Hull. Since then, about $450 million in federal funds have been invested in glossy office buildings and a whole constellation of development and today nearly 13,000 civil servants pour into Hull each day, with another 9,000 to follow within the next couple of years.

Ultimately — possibly within five years — the pulp and paper mill will be relocated as well, and the river front will be transformed into a paradise of parks and shops and brand new homes. Hull has become a federally-funded battleground for the hearts of her people.

But it hasn't worked. In Quebec, as everywhere, people are preoccupied with earning a living. Certainly the people of Hull have been economically blessed. But the massive infusion of money was inevitably accompanied by English-speaking citizens upsetting the balance, diluting the French character of the area. One report indicated that more than half the new residents were English-speaking civil servants.

The people of Hull voted several Péquistes into office in the Nov. 15, 1976 election including Jocelyn Oullette, now the province's minister of public works.

A few weeks after I passed through the area, Jean Alfred, a Parti Québécois member of the Quebec National Assembly, charged the federal government with plotting "cultural genocide" in Hull, with conspiracy "to anglicize the Outaouais region by the invasion of federal buildings in which 95 per cent of the civil servants are unilingual English."

Walter Baker, Progressive Conservative Member of Parliament for Grenville-Carleton, has watched the situation closely and I asked him how he viewed the squabble. He spoke of the collision between the National Capital Commission (Ottawa) and the regional government of Outaouais and said that if Quebec were to secede "there'd have to be some settlement of assets . . . it would be a lawyer's dream. The lawyers shall inherit the earth."

Truly, the legal fees involved in divvying up close to half a billion dollars worth of development would be astronomical, but I was disturbed by his calm acceptance of the possibility of separation. He had not only sampled his own constituents, but he had also traveled across Canada. "The attitudes across the country run from 'to hell with them' to 'ho hum'," he told me. "I don't find people standing up on their hind legs waving flags. I get very little mail on national unity and I was getting piles of it at one stage. I'm very fearful of the spirit. I don't know whether we're capable of whipping ourselves up into some great national euphoric state of mind."

Shortly after the PQ victory in Quebec, Baker circulated a questionnaire in his riding. The returns were very high — 25 per cent compared to a normal 9 per cent — and "there was a healthy suspicion developing about the national unity business. Everybody wanted Quebec to stay in Confederation, everybody felt that the people of Quebec wanted to stay in Confederation. But when it came to the question of special status for Quebec it dropped to 50 per cent."

His report confirmed some of the doubts I had acquired. If not doubts about Canada's future, then an alarming absence of certainty that we could maintain the status quo. Nor did I feel quite so positive that we should even try, but more of that later. For the moment I was about to encounter Quebec and as the bus rolled into Montreal I found I was dreading it.

Always, when I arrive at a destination, I experience a disconcerting sense of disorientation. It's an uncomfortable feeling which can last from a few minutes to a few days. In Montreal it generally lasts until I leave; it's a city I've never been able to come to terms with. Obviously this has much to do with the fact that I don't speak French but it goes deeper than that. I feel more comfortable in Quebec City than I do in Montreal. In Montreal I feel I am encroaching. In Quebec City I feel I am visiting. I have friends in Montreal, and family, and no reason to feel alone but there is always that gnawing sense of intruding. I've been visiting the city since my early teens and more recently, for a period of two years, traveling there almost weekly. In those days I had absolutely no sense of having flown 350 miles, of crossing a provincial boundary, and I rarely detected much cultural change. It had merely taken me two hours to get to work that day instead of twenty-five or thirty minutes by bus and subway in Toronto.

Montreal had become an extension of Toronto in my mind. Living in Toronto you become so used to hearing other languages spoken that you simply tune them out. In Montreal there is only French to tune out and often, if you're travelling on business, not much of that. The difference between Place Ville Marie and the Toronto Dominion Centre is negligible; for all I know or care they could have come from the same architect's drawing board. And yet, at another level I am conscious of the uneasy co-existence of two disparate and increasingly antagonistic cultures. It's disturbing and I resent it, but being unilingual makes it difficult to come to grips with Quebec.

I don't feel guilty about not speaking French. I feel angry, cheated, exasperated and, as a journalist, isolated. And sometimes despised.

Once I had this forcibly thrust on me. I had been assigned to write an article about the enormous hydro-electric project near Fort George on the Quebec side of James Bay. A series of dams across La Grande River was being built and I had dealings with some Hydro Quebec public relations officials prior to visiting the construction sites. Two of the public relations men, accompanied by a staff biologist, took me to lunch. We had spent the morning discussing plans for my tour and of course we spoke English, but when we entered the restaurant the three of them switched to French, utterly ignoring me: a stinging rebuke to the *anglais* writer from Toronto. It was like a sixty-minute slap in the face.

When we returned to the office we spoke English again but I was seething with anger and humiliation.

I LEARNED TO milk a cow at a farm just outside of Lotbinière when I was a boy. The man who taught me — his name was Dupont — spoke few words of English and was very patient with me. There was a boy my own age on the farm and he and I communicated for a week, entirely in sign language. We became good friends and we "talked" incessantly. There was an accident on the highway one day and Luc came dashing to find me. He mimed the whole story — two cars had collided, no one was seriously hurt but the cars were a mess and one of the drivers was blind drunk — almost as fast as he could have spoken about it.

Once I spent an evening with a French Canadian in Minnesota. His English was as bad as my French and we experimented with both, laughing, telling stories, singing, ultimately pledging eternal friendship and exchanging telephone numbers and addresses which, of course, we lost. I was on assignment; he was there for a snowmobile sales convention. He lived in Montreal.

Language is not the barrier; it is the attitude that forms the barrier — or eliminates it. There are people who have spent their whole lives in Toronto speaking neither English nor French. My next door neighbors are Chinese and speak English as well as I do, but the grandparents speak only a few words. The old man was running a laundry on Yonge Street near my home when I was a boy. He's retired now and must have done reasonably well; he drives a good car and has a good home; he smiles when he sees me and we exchange remarks about the weather. He looks happy. Friendly. We share this city, this country amicably, he and I. I am no threat to him; he is no threat to me. His legacy to Canada is a close-knit family, hardworking and pleasant, the children headed for university. Toronto's residents are Portuguese, Dutch, Italian, Greek, German and all the rest. It makes an interesting and cosmopolitan city.

Why, then, can I never relax and enjoy Montreal? Sometimes when I walk along St. Catherine Street people will smile at me and nod a friendly hello, something that just doesn't happen in Toronto. One dines well in both cities but it seems more leisurely in Montreal. A friend once told me that Toronto, Chicago and New York are masculine cities where goods are manufactured and business is transacted. Montreal, San Francisco and New Orleans are feminine cities more in tune with caprice and beauty, the central preoccupation being the enjoyment of life and business and industry merely the means to an end. I liked that.

NOW I FOUND myself more reluctant than ever to penetrate Montreal, the city I'd like to love but where, more and more, I feel alien, a foreigner.

I quit the bus and deposited my suitcase in a locker. Everything I would need for the next few days was stuffed into my flight bag or pockets. I had some shopping to do but plenty of time — my cousin and his wife wouldn't be expecting me until dinner time — and I headed first for the lounge.

The man next to me spoke, in heavily accented and broken English and asked me where I was from, what I was doing and we talked for a while. Yes, I was married and had three sons; yes, it was a long trip by bus, a long time to be away from home but an occupational hazard. He looked at me rather owlishly, and when he spoke it was with genuine concern. "But what," he asked, "about your sex life?"

At first I was stunned. Then I burst out laughing, trying to speak but totally incapable. True absurdity is a thing to be cherished. At last I stopped and assured him, to the best of my ability, that I thought I could survive a brief period of celibacy. It was not, after all, like giving up smoking. He seemed dubious about that but didn't press it. I looked at him closely for the first time: paunchy, mid-fifties, slightly drunk and highly, *outrageously* inquisitive. Shortly after, I left, in much better humor than I had been on arrival.

Here I was, a typically uptight *anglais* trying to determine if and why my country was about to self-destruct and the first Quebecker I meet is concerned about my sex life. It was too much. It reminded me of a nasty story I'd heard somewhere about a French Canadian who had gone to work for an Alberta farmer. After about a year they had become friends and were talking and the farmer says, "Pierre, how is it that collectively French Canadians are such a bunch of bastards but guys like you, you're so nice?"

"I don't know," says Pierre. "How come the opposite's true in your case?"

I went shopping. There was some difficulty over the underwear. "Box-air shorts?" The salesgirl shrugged so I just hunted until I found a pair. Tapes, typing paper, toothbrush

(I'd left it behind in North Bay) and since it was drizzling outside I considered an umbrella but decided against it. I hate carrying things when I'm traveling and I'd managed to get halfway across a continent with neither raincoat nor umbrella; perhaps the rain would stop. It generally, does, eventually.

I found a cab and jumped in, giving the driver my cousin's address in Westmount, watching to see if his lips would tighten in contempt. They didn't so I assumed he was English but he was Greek and I decided I was getting paranoid about the whole thing.

Dinner, conversation, children playing. Sometimes family relationships become friendships as well and I basked in the pleasure of being if not home, welcome. Bed. The problems of the nation could wait until morning. Fairly late in the morning, please.

IN FACT IT wasn't until mid-afternoon that I found myself climbing the steep hill to Purvis Hall, at the corner of Pine and Peel Streets, to listen to Dale Thompson, one of the more temperate and articulate spokesmen for Montreal's English-speaking minority. Thompson teaches political science at the University of Montreal and McGill, and is a former vice-president of McGill. Currently he is president of the Westmount Municipal Association. He was born in Alberta "at a little place called Fort Assiniboine, which is a farming community about a hundred miles northwest of Edmonton on the Athabasca River. My brother has the farm and I still feel I have my roots there. I had a little fun a couple of weeks ago when they elected me head of the Westmount association by having myself introduced as a western farm boy. It amuses me because Westmount is really a pretty phoney myth about the Anglophone establishment . . . people use it as a convenient target . . .''

Thompson studied French at university, studied in France, worked in Chicoutimi, taught in French at the University of Montreal for thirteen years, spent four years working as secretary to Prime Minister Louis St. Laurent. At the moment most of his work is done in French. He is a quiet, soft-spoken man, suitably professorial in demeanor. In fact he spoke so dispassionately, with such detachment, that when I studied the transcript of our meeting I found myself astonished by the bluntness of expression, the harshness of judgment, the odd ability to discuss a question in both hypothetical and real terms, often with totally separate, almost contradictory attitudes. He describes himself as a liberal democrat and when I asked what that involved he said, "It means essentially to me that the individual is more important than the collectivity, and that the state is at the service of the individual. I have no qualms about voting against or speaking against the Liberals." In fact he voted Liberal in the Lévesque election "but it was one of the toughest votes I ever cast. I cursed myself all the way up the steps. I wanted to vote for someone who had some principles and I found the Bourassa team had no principles at all. I think not more than twenty per cent voted for separatism, the others voted in sheer frustration against Bourassa. I think the polls indicated immediately after the election that the people said 'My God, that isn't what we really wanted to do; we wanted to kick Bourassa out or we wanted to teach him a lesson. We're not against the Liberals, we just thought they had a bad team and ought to start over again.'

"That's what the Liberals should have done, they should have kicked out Bourassa and put the election back for a year, which they could have done, and I think they wouldn't have been too badly off. Once the thing had happened, a lot of my friends said 'We didn't really mean it, don't get excited about it, we'll turf René Lévesque out next time unless he absolutely rejects separatism.'

"Which he can never afford to do, and I don't think he's inclined to, either."

Thompson has little patience for the cultural aspects of the row in Quebec, little regard for the reasoning of Lévesque's team (although this is tinged with admiration for the political strategies involved). "I challenge this terminology which they use," he told me, "this notion — which doesn't stand up scientifically in my view — that because people speak one language they learn to think in a certain way, which forms their minds, and a culture emanates from that language. That they are then a nation and every nation deserves a state; a nation state deserves its own independence and the only way to have peace in the world is for every language, which is a culture, which is a nation, which is a state to have its own organization. And of course this is bloody nonsense.''

My mind was beginning to spin, and to slow him down I asked what he thought would happen next. It was, of course, a futile effort on my part and I was glad the little tape recorder sat on the desk between us as I checked nervously from time to time to make sure the cassette spindles were turning.

"Well," he said, "I think it's too early to say. First, the language bill is going to go through with some minor modifications, simply because that's the way parliamentary democracy works. They've got seventy members. The Liberals will put up a pretty good fight. The Union Nationale won't put up much of a fight because they're concerned about their national image. They realize that the majority of French Canadians are not unhappy about the bill and they're going to try to squeeze the Liberals out of second place in the assembly during the next election . . .

"I said the majority of French Canadians are not unhappy about the bill and I think that's quite true because the surveys indicate that thirty per cent of French Canadians don't read many papers at all, and a number read no papers except the local French press, so they're not getting any of the anti arguments . . .

"And the legislation gives them priority in all jobs, as far as they can tell. What they're not able to see sufficiently is that there's no point in having legislation to give them priority for a job if the job no longer exists. There's the catch, and that's the kind of argument that hasn't been getting through to them.

"I think the Parti Québécois government is very clever. I think they've got a very good strategy as I understand it. They've managed to keep the federalists off balance. You hardly dare say you're a federalist around this province, particularly if you're a French Canadian. I'm a federalist but that's a different matter. I've never identified with French Canadians, Westmount, English Canadians, Western Canadians or anything else, so there's no problem for me.

"But for someone who has a group identity, particularly a French Canadian, this poses a very serious problem. After the election, about seventy per cent of French Canadians said they felt good about it, a good assertion of their own personality, and if one took a position against that, he was likely to be considered anti-French Canadian. So the PQ has been very good, very clever . . .

"The surveys also indicated that somewhere between eight and twenty per cent of French Canadians now feel confident enough to go it on their own. They don't believe the scare tactics about economic deprivations and so on. They just feel 'OK, let's go, we can ride this thing out, we can solve our problems.' And so they could, in the long run. But the polls also indicated that fifty per cent of the people are more interested in the economics than the culture of the question. Culture is really a buzzword for jobs. So if people talk culture they mean jobs. So what we really need to do is demonstrate more clearly that Canada is a valid economic unit."

I stopped him again. "Did you say you thought Quebec could go it alone?"

"Oh sure, I've always felt that."

"What about the rest of the country?"

"The rest of the country can make it, too. Oh it would mean a lot of inconvenience and a lot of disruption but there wouldn't be anything very serious . . . . The only difference would be that they (French Canadians) would have some kind of say in determining the economic policy of all the country, or at least as far as it affected them. And I don't think it would be possible to have a different currency . . ."

A professor of political science who thinks it could work?

"Well I was just responding to your questions about whether this is economically viable, which is almost an academic question. If I were to draw a scenario of what might really happen I'd say they'd go ahead with the referendum. I think the question would be 'sovereignty association'. If it gets too wishy-washy, not enough independence in it, the Federal Government will simply say in advance it wouldn't recognize this as a legitimate question, and that will influence the voters. So I think that in those conditions of uncertainty the public might say — and don't forget that Trudeau is just as popular in this province as Lévesque, in fact the polls say he's more popular — get on back, you guys and sit down and see if you can get along together. Work something out that's in the interests of Quebec. And they'd turn down the referendum on those grounds.''

I told Thompson that I saw René Lévesque as a politician of great integrity. I intended to expand, postulating that he could become the catalyst that would force us to resolve our national problems once and for all but he cut me off.

"Integrity?'' he said. "I'm not so sure that word buys too much in this circumstance. He's a man who's got an *idée fixe*. He's not very interested in a wide range of subjects. He's hooked on this separatist thing. He hated the English for what they did when he was a kid in New Carlyle. He was raised in a community where the French Canadians were the working class, and he developed this very strong resentment which he still has today . . . . But there's one thing that's true; there's a natural alliance with René Lévesque and a broad sector of the population.

"Ever since there's been any kind of a legislative system, going back to the Constitutional Act, people have used it in this province very cleverly to get better conditions for French Canadians. That's really what the history of parliamentary assemblies has been in the province of Quebec. A minority learns to use these things in a very clever way. You've got a separatist government and they're playing on a kind of guilt complex, idealism, uncertainties, self-interest, a whole combination of things in order to get the best possible deal they can. My guess is that we can get into a situation where it will not be in their interests to vote separatist. They're not interested in separatism they're interested in better conditions for themselves.''

Jobs. Everywhere I went in Canada it all boiled down to jobs. It becomes a bit more complex than that in Quebec but the essence remains. The people don't want to feel like foreigners in Canada and I don't want to feel like a foreigner when I'm in Quebec. What do French Canadians need?

"Well, they're a 200-year-old minority and what they want is maximum security, security of employment, and that means employment in their own language. That's why they talk about linguistic and cultural security. There are all kinds of psychoses which they're not happy about — the kind of psychosis that Lévesque has, and the others. So people like Claude Castonguay, whom I happen to admire, say 'Let's see how far we can go to cure this complex for this minority situation and see if there isn't a situation where we can all live together to our mutual advantage.' I guess that's what I'm all about, too."

Thompson agreed that the British North America Act needs revision. "The constitutional question is important," he said. "We'll have to get round to that one of these days. Mind you there's an awful lot of nonsense talked about it. For instance in the *Canadian Forum* there was a kind of declaration calling for a new constitution or something, and if you read it it's really the most effete kind of academism that you can possibly imagine. Sort of saying 'We expect the French Canadians to do what they want. We'd like to think they'll remain in Canada, it's really up to them. We'll do anything we can to make that possible.' Well you don't deal with an independent group in that particular way. You try to find a just solution. They're not going to discuss the constitution until the principle of Quebec's sovereignty has been accepted and that knocks this Toronto do-goody intellectual attitude into a cocked hat because how are you going to discuss with somebody what you can do to give them what they want when, in effect, what they want is independence?

"What we *can* do is develop a series of proposals, a series of arguments and a series of benefits for French Canadians to give them a greater degree of security, so that at some stage they'll say 'All right, René Lévesque, you have been very useful to us, you have helped us to get a much better deal. If this is written into firm guarantees we think we'll stay within Canada . . .' That's about as good a scenario as I can imagine.

"You know," he mused, "René Lévesque is not a very

ambitious man. It's an interesting thing, but all the time he was in the wilderness he was saying, 'I wish I could get out of this, I don't really care about all this kind of stuff anyway.' You could almost feel that somewhere there might be an excuse for him to step down from the leadership. Lead a more relaxed, a more Bohemian life. Think he likes getting up at eight o'clock in the morning? Not René Lévesque.

"The French Canadian has broken out much less than I would have expected fifteen years ago when I was teaching at the University of Montreal," he continued. "It seems to me that the separatists are perpetuating a situation rather than doing anything about it, by these intellectual arguments; by saying 'you are a nation, therefore you are a people' and not by giving the counter-argument that there are 2,500 languages in the world and practically every country has more than one language. And that what we have to learn is to co-exist and not worry about multiplying the number of states."

Much of what Thompson said seemed to tie in with what I'd been hearing on the prairies and I mentioned this, that many people I had talked with thought that the people of Quebec were very surprised when they found they'd elected Lévesque. Thompson chuckled with almost malicious glee. "So was he," he said.

We talked for a long time and maybe it was partly because he envied me not only my trip across Canada, which he admitted, but also my freedom as a non-academic to simply write about the people I met. "That's where your project could be interesting to me," he said, "because you don't have to do these broad generalizations, you can talk on a human level."

He wound up with a few broadsides, generalizations of his own. The mood of Quebec today? "Can't generalize," he said. "Certainly there's a lot of concern, a tough attitude, a we-will-fight attitude and this is a very dangerous thing. Violence is closer to the surface of human beings than a lot of people care to admit."

Leadership? A vacuum. "There's no English Canadian leadership. Granted, the Liberals have Pierre but they'd like to have John Turner. I never saw a situation so ripe for leadership. John's too cautious. He wouldn't give that kind of leadership. You know those hard decisions that Lincoln agonized about? John would come down with some wishy-washy formula."

National priorities? "I'd put the economy at the top. Solve the economics and you'd solve a lot of the other problems."

Unemployment? "About nine per cent in Quebec, the same as British Columbia. Many French Canadians are ill-equipped, ill-trained, paper-trained but not competent and there's no proper work for them. This year there were 2,500 applications for law schools. If we took them all you'd have 1,500 unemployed lawyers. Also, the French Canadians haven't swung into new fields — technology and commerce — and until they do we aren't going to solve economic problems. Kids still want the professions — doctors, lawyers, university professors. They don't want to become chemical engineers, business administrators, technicians, people who can fix cars or telephones or plumbing — the down-to-earth things."

I said I'd read somewhere that the Americans are suffering from "a surfeit of democracy" and asked if he felt that applied to us. He said there is a difficulty. "Once a person gets elected, he's immediately got a stake in climbing up that greasy pole in Ottawa and so, quite often, he puts his career ahead of his regional interests. There has to be somebody reminding him that he's supposed to be there representing the people . . . . I prefer to see mature people in politics rather than young people. Mature people aren't going anywhere. Someone who doesn't really need the job. Younger people are too intent on their careers. Stanfield wasn't mistrusted in Quebec, he just couldn't compete with Trudeau. It's the party that was mistrusted. Tories here are not a grass roots organization."

W E PARTED, and I walked down the hill toward the Four Seasons Hotel, where I was meeting a friend for a drink. She was late and I sat waiting, reflecting on Dale Thompson's ideas and activities. He'd just completed his own brief opposing Bill One (in French, of course) and the local papers were grousing about a 90-minute limit the Government had imposed on briefs to be presented during the language bill hearings. Thompson suspected there'd be about 150 of them and my sympathies lay, I'm afraid, with the Government.

Then I stopped thinking about anything at all, and suddenly it occurred to me again, my Montreal malaise, and one of the contributing factors: the Four Seasons. Place Ville Marie. The new Eaton Centre in Toronto. I could be blindfolded and deposited in a convention hotel lobby and I wouldn't know whether I was in Toronto, Montreal, London or somewhere in the mid-western United States. Maybe that's what scares the French Canadians: North American homogeneity. It scares me too. Do they see themselves as a minority of six million French-speaking people surrounded by 250 million materialistic, technology-oriented English-speaking members of a continental community? Don't they understand? Can't they comprehend that I feel the same way? I too, fear cultural domination by that enormous conglomerate south of us. Surely we have some common bond there, the French Canadian and I.

My friend walked in. We used to work together and we spent most of the time gossiping, reminiscing. She mentioned that she, like me, felt uncomfortable in Montreal despite the fact that she'd been living there for several years. I sympathized, saying it must be difficult if you don't speak French and she looked at me with astonishment. "John," she said, "I speak *fluent* French, didn't you know?" No, I'd made the silly assumption that because she came originally from Australia she, like me, would speak only English. She'd learned the language in France, before she came to Canada.

And that brought me back to my original point, or rather the corollary to it; that if ignorance of the language isn't the barrier, neither is speaking it necessarily the bridge. More and more I think this language thing is a red herring, something we can easily live with. It was another point I'd raised with Dale Thompson and later I replayed the tape. I had asked him about bilingualism and he said "I don't think it's a practical proposition. That's why Trudeau has gone to such pains in speeches like the one he made in Saskatchewan, that he doesn't think it necessary. I certainly don't feel that my neighbors in Fort Assiniboine, Alberta, should have to be bilingual, although I feel it would be good for them. What I think is needed at the present time is a competence to evaluate what human beings really need, over and above all the propaganda and clichés and buzzwords. If we could somehow get at what they're really concerned about . . . ."

THE SHOULDER strap on my flight bag had broken earlier that day and I'd taken it to Tony's Shoe Repair Shop in Westmount.

Tony's is one of the Westmount symbols writers like to single out, a crowded little shop where limousines may stop, a liveried chauffeur carrying milady's shoes in for repair. I suppose that it does happen occasionally, too.

I suppose, too, that Westmount will forever remain a symbol of English domination of the French. It's a community of 22,000 people today, ranging from the very rich at the top of the 530-foot "mountain" to the increasingly modest middle-class homes below. A fifth of the people living there today are French, perhaps a quarter or more are English and the rest are a polyglot of ethnic diversity hardly deserving the harsh epithet used by Keith Spicer, when he was still Canada's Official Languages Commissioner. In the words of *Canadian Magazine* writer, Robert Stewart, Spicer, wanting a symbol for Anglophone resistance to Canada's French Fact, "used René Lévesque's 'Westmount Rhodesians' phrase. In retrospect, Spicer said he hadn't meant it seriously. But nonetheless, it reflects the anti-French image of Westmount in many Canadians' minds."

But the British Bastion theory doesn't hold water anymore, or not very much. And the people I know who live in Westmount are fluently bilingual and quite conscious of the so-called French Fact.

There is also the English Fact, and it isn't centered in

Westmount. There are more than a million people in Quebec who speak only English and life may not be easy for them in the next few years. There are *à vendre* signs everywhere, as people try to extricate themselves from the province, and I'm told you can't rent a safety deposit box in any bank east of Cornwall, because people are caching their possessions in the safety of good old Ontario. I've no idea whether this is true, it's just part of the lore. Nasty stories. "How does a smart Montreal businessman talk to a dumb Montreal businessman? By long distance telephone."

This sort of thing can get out of hand. And yes, I've read that dreadful, best-selling paranoid pocket book *Bilingual Today, French Tomorrow*, wherein a retired naval officer exposes Trudeau's conspiratorial plot to turn Canada into a French nation. It's nonsense. There's nothing new in playing on the fears of the people during times of political uncertainty. There was a German house-painter who made quite a name for himself with such polemics.

I DINED WITH a French Canadian journalist I'd met, a man who seems at first to be hostile to English Canada, but who is nonetheless a moderate in the Quebec political spectrum of today. He is annoyed with us and expresses his feelings pungently but I do not think he is a separatist — he's much too rational for that.

We talked at first about the differences that exist between French and English language newspapering. It interested me that one French newspaper's reporters are consulted on matters of editorial policy, something I cannot conceive of happening on any of the newspapers or magazines I have worked for.

Perhaps because we did not know each other well, perhaps because he was diplomatic by nature, he treated me with more courtesy than I am used to from my colleagues. I tried to respond to this but was distracted by the things we discussed and soon became blunt-spoken; he may have found me abrasive. He sat across the table, enjoying his dinner, and I examined him. He fit no newsroom stereotype: rumpled in dress and demeanor, thick black untamed beard, precise and almost pedantic in conversation. A school teacher, maybe. A gentleman.

He made me very angry.

I told him what I'd been doing and said I was trying to understand why "separatism" is such an inflammatory word in Quebec, while it seems both fair and accurate at home.

"Look," he said with some intensity, "if I am a politician, and I say I want to nationalize the hydro, would you call me a communist?"

"Of course not," I said, "but you aren't trying to na-tionalize the hydro, you've already done that. You're threatening to separate, to secede, from Canada."

Well, he tried to explain it to me and I tried to understand and after a while he gave up, trying instead to explain what is meant by "sovereignty association." That didn't work either, not because I don't understand it but because I'm far from sure it can be sold to English Canada. Then he tried another ploy, the analogy with a broken marriage. It seemed an impossibly Gallic solution but here it is, as closely as I can reconstruct it.

Suppose a husband and wife realize that their marriage has failed, or that it no longer satisfies either partner. However, neither partner plans remarriage and while the love may have ended there is no great animosity. Furthermore, there are children. There is a home. There is much shared experience and much commonality of interest.

Suppose they decide against divorce, find a legal separation prohibitively costly and complicated. Instead, being mature, twentieth century people, they decide to maintain their relationship pretty much as it is, but with some important modifications. They continue with a mutually acceptable division of labor and responsibilities. Certain parts of the home remain common ground.

But they bring in a contractor who alters the house, to provide two separate bedrooms, each with separate doors leading to the street. The partnership remains unchanged as far as the children are concerned, as far as the business of living is concerned, perhaps even as far as dining and entertaining are concerned.

At day's end, both are free to entertain whatever companions they desire, with adequate provisions for privacy.

At this point I was feeling a trifle ill. I could see the practicality of the arrangement. Logical and, in many respects, desirable. There was just one problem. I cannot conceive of such an arrangement working out satisfactorily. I just don't think human nature — my own nature — would permit it.

I was more than a little chagrined. First of all, I felt threatened by the scheme in a way that I didn't like to admit, even to myself. Secondly, I'd demonstrated to myself, at least, that I was emotionally incapable of participating in the kind of dialogue that may become necessary.

In fairness I must add that there had been more conversation before this analogy was raised, enough to tell me that the man was not himself a separatist, or at least not necessarily one. He was aware, however, of the attitudes of his people and was trying to give me some sort of insight into the difference between us. In that I fear he was chillingly successful. In retrospect, I believe he was a federalist, as much committed to Confederation as I am. For different reasons, perhaps. I suppose I should be grateful to him and maybe I am.

I HAD LUNCH that day with a unilingual English-speaking acquaintance who has for some time watched Quebec politics closely. He spoke bluntly of the Péquistes and "the politics of vengeance". I found him opinionated and a little unnerving.

"It really is the politics of vengeance," he said. "They are, to their credit perhaps, a socialist party. The Parti Québécois has never been favorably disposed toward big business. People seem surprised when such businesses move out. It doesn't surprise me. They have a mildly socialistic policy which they're going to implement. And I think it's naive to suppose that they're not acting as though separation had already taken place. They're not giving us good government, reform government, they're acting as though they'd won the referendum for independence. I don't think Trudeau will find it at all easy dealing with these people. The generation now in school will be indoctrinated to accept a separatist viewpoint."

"You seem to regard secession as likely," I said.

"Oh, certainly I do. It's a possibility and until English Canadians realize that, there are a lot of scores that will have to be settled."

In December, 1958, when René Lévesque was making a name for himself as a shrewd and sharp-tongued broadcast journalist, seventy-four French language television and radio producers voted to strike against *Radio Canada*, the French language arm of the CBC. Their English-speaking counterparts in Toronto, after a brief stoppage, returned to their jobs. Lévesque, although not himself a producer, became deeply involved in the politics and leadership of the strike. He became politicized at that time, and embittered, as he told his biographer, Peter Desbarats: "I never quite got over it . . . I learned then that French was really very secondary in the rest of Canada's mind, certainly in Ottawa's."

My lunch guest continued: "The CBC strike left an enormous scar on Lévesque's psyche and now people who support him are lashing back. I find it most ironical that, if you look at the PQ Cabinet, practically all of them are bilingual, practically all of them have been educated at Harvard, the Massachusetts Institute of Technology, the Sorbonne or the London School of Economics. They are elitists who've got to where they are because they are fluently bilingual. And they're trying to impose a ghetto culture on working class people which is a culture their own lifestyles aren't aligned with. There's an element of hypocrisy there. They've gotten to where they are now because their eyes and their consciousness have been opened to the rest of the world, and yet they don't want for their own people what they've had for themselves."

He was contemptuous of Robert Bourassa for calling the election. "It was a totally phoney election on an incomprehensible issue. I'm not surprised he lost. The interesting thing is this guy Rodrigue Biron of the Union Nationale. He's a formidable guy, a very right wing guy waiting in the wings to reimpose a Duplessis-type order if the Parti Québécois screws up the next election."

"Do you think they will?"

"Oh yeah, I think the question is who do you blame for unemployment, and Biron talks privately about seventeen per cent unemployment within the next eighteen months. Worse than depression. You can blame unemployment on the PQ to some extent because they're driving some major corporations out of Quebec. The mood of the Anglophone community is one of apprehension. The Francophone community is harder to stereotype. Most of them have an element of pride in what they think the PQ will achieve for them but that doesn't mean they support their doctrine or their dogma . . . . My own prognosis is that there's going to be three or four more years of uncertainty and economic stagnation. And if I were Trudeau I'd call a federal election as soon as possible to resolve this. I think if he did he could win practically every riding in Quebec. French Canadians have been schizoid about their politics for a long time. Same with Ontario, for that matter."

The question is whether the average Montrealer can stand four years of continuing political crisis. "I'm talking psychologically now. The emotional tension is terrific. There's more drinking, which is probably a good release. But can racial tensions be contained so that you don't end up with an Ulster situation or a Cyprus situation? If demagogues come to the fore, that will be it.

"Look, for all sorts of philosophical reasons, the dedicated PQ supporter thinks in group or collective terms. The Anglophone thinks in terms of individual rights. So on Bill One Camille Laurin (Minister for Cultural Development and author of the controversial language charter) — he's an honest man — talks about the collectivity of French Quebec. Anglophones talk about the right of the individual Greek cafe owner to display a sign in any language he chooses. It's a basic philosophical difference between a corporate or collective ideology and an individualist one. It's hard to get Francophones or Anglophones to accept this. They don't use the same philosophical terms. Separatism is a bad word in French. In English it's a very simple declarative of what might happen if Quebec left Canada, so it's partly a matter of semantics . . .

sovereignty association is a popular term now. It implies more than state's rights — you're talking about a sovereign state which would have some economic attachment with what remained of Canada. The argument is based on a totally false analogy, the European Common Market. They [the Péquistes] don't understand that the state has to *yield* sovereignty in order to belong to the common market. Housewives in Britain have their butter prices dictated by Brussels. The EEC bureaucracy. So here you've got this incredible flaw in the Parti Québécois logic, that you can have your cake and eat it too. You either want total political sovereignty, which means you go it alone, or you want economic association with the rest of Canada, and if you have that, you can't call all the shots.''

It is this desire for economic sovereignty that bothers English Canadians most, the idea that Quebec should be able to govern itself independent of the rest of Canada, but at the same time enjoy a sheltered economy, protected by the rest of the country. Invariably the response is an acrimonious and emotional one: Why the hell should we support a separate Quebec? English Canadians I have spoken to say it sounds like a man paying alimony to a wife who has deserted, taking much of what he owned away with her.

Another paradox. My companion thinks Lévesque's personal philosophy is close to the Anglophone attitude, which tends to respect individual over collective rights. The men surrounding Lévesque, my companion feels, would sacrifice individual rights for what they see as the general good of the province as a separate whole. He continued: ''It may be we'll realize one day that the Lévesque election was good, because the confrontation, the conflict will be a bloodless one by politicians and bureaucrats. A protracted constitutional hassle. It may sound awfully banal, but in this province today a majority opposes secession and the worst possible thing that could happen would be that the rest of Canada could say 'to hell with you' and abandon all those Francophones who still believe in Canada. That is the great, possible tragedy.''

H E HAD TWO other points to make, both of them, I think, as critically important as this last. The first has to do with the fact that economics, despite its impact on our daily lives, is an incomprehensible and utterly boring field for the mass of people. "We're dealing with a question of economic co-operation in a country called Canada which is a very boring subject." But crucial to our future. "Look what happened in Europe. Germany, France and Britain have historically been enemies, have killed millions of people because of their troubles. Now they're yielding sovereignty to the central authority of the European Common Market for the common good of their people. You try making that story interesting. In my view the best means of survival lies in having a bigger economy of scale, larger units."

I found myself recalling my days as Washington correspondent for the *Toronto Telegram*. For two years — the last two years of the Lyndon Johnson administration — I covered everything. Assassinations. Race riots. Anti-war demonstrations. Space shots. Banner headlines several times a week. Then the Nixon administration moved in and things quieted down and suddenly — remember, this was long before Watergate — I had to absorb whole new disciplines. Energy. Fiscal policy. Auto pacts. Balance of payments. These were stories that had far more impact on the individual Canadian's life than space shots and race riots, but they were boring stories: boring to research, boring to write, boring to read. But vitally important. It's one of the unsolvable paradoxes of journalism.

The second, and final point he raised was something I'd already begun to sense. "Maybe," he said, "the issue facing Quebec now — and I know what the separatist answer is because I've discussed it — is this: are you prepared to lower your standard of living *appreciably* for independence? We're talking about ordinary people, nine per cent, ten per cent of whom don't have goddam jobs right now. You're talking about them lowering their standard of living for the luxury — and it's a very beautiful luxury, a wonderful concept — of nationalism? You're telling them they're going to pay a price. But the politicians and the bureaucrats never pay the price. They ride around in their limousines. They're asking the little man, who's been put upon for too long in this world, to pay a very heavy price for the symbolical trappings of independence. *It's elitist, limousine-radicalism.*

"It's also the question facing the rest of Canada. All of Canada. Are we willing to pay the price to keep the nation together? It's a very stiff price. You can start by doubling whatever you're paying for automobile gasoline and go on from there. But the *real* question, I think, is can we afford not to pay that price. There are separatist groups from coast to coast who are so put off by the inequities of the century-old British North America Act, by the blatant self-interest of Ottawa's politicians and bureaucrats, that they think they can go it alone."

And so they can. And so can any third world country, any fifth rate banana republic. The problem is that we can't grow bananas, not with our climate. And we can't pretend to impoverishment, we're too goddamned big, too rich in resources while half the world is starving. If we fragment it won't last for long. We'll be swallowed up by someone, perhaps the Americans; perhaps we'd be carved up by a triumvirate of super powers.

And the first thing we'd lose would be our freedom. We're one of the last surviving democracies extant in the world today. We could lose that.

D INNER THAT NIGHT with two friends, both writers, former co-workers. They began talking about the Eleventh Province mob and so it was that I discovered there are at least three "eleventh" provinces currently being proposed for Canada. One, of course, is Ed Deibel's plan to split northern Ontario away from the south. Another is more of a gesture than a movement; a handful of Newfoundland MLAs want to declare Labrador a province. I think there are about 40,000 people in Labrador but they're sitting on a lot of minerals and a lot of hydro-electric potential and they're being systematically robbed of both.

The third — and the only one that actually calls itself the "Committee for an 11th Province" — is a well-financed Anglophone backlash movement which would create an English-speaking province called West Quebec. I will attempt to treat it with all due respect but I have to confess that I class it a few notches above that awful little pocket book, *Bilingual Today, French Tomorrow*. That is to say I find it paranoid, pessimistic and of little positive value to the national debate. Never mind, that's only one man's opinion.

The "Eleventh" province would, of course, be the tenth province by default, since it would only come into being (or attempt to do so) if and when Quebec seceded, at which point Canada would comprise just nine provinces with an emerging nation in their midst. It has been called the brainchild of Dr. William Shaw, Union Nationale MNA from Pointe Claire, a suburb of Montreal. Shaw demurs, saying this is giving him more credit than is due; that the matter was discussed way back in 1966 by a university professor named Pierre Elliott Trudeau. The closest I've been able to come to verifying that is that Lionel Albert, one of the committee members, claimed Trudeau had written that "once the inviolability of Canada has been questioned, so the inviolability of Quebec can be questioned."

In any event the scheme is by no means modest. Shaw and his colleagues would, in the event of secession of Quebec, proclaim the Province of West Quebec. It would include that portion of Quebec lying south of the St. Lawrence River, stretching from the Ontario border to New Brunswick; it would take in the city of Hull, including the Gatineau Valley, plus the west end of the island of Montreal. It would leave the renegade nation of Quebec with most of the city of Montreal; its capital, Quebec City; a lot of boreal forest and some pretty good skiing.

Dr. Shaw's own leader, the Union Nationale's Rodrigue Biron, has several times rapped his maverick backbencher's knuckles and the doctor has recently stepped down as leader of the movement. I don't know why.

West Quebec would, of course, be bilingual according to its promoters, although I can't help thinking that a French-speaking person might be very uncomfortable living there. Shaw, for example, is himself bilingual but always speaks English in the Quebec National Assembly, just to remind his fellow members of the English Fact.

Meetings began soon after the Lévesque election and by the end of January they were calling themselves the Preparatory Committee for the Eleventh Province. By mid-March this had become the Provisional Committee for an Eleventh Province and by the end of May, committee member Rudy Loesser was campaigning for funds for his war chest.

According to some reports, the original idea did come from Dr. Shaw, who argued that those parts of Quebec which vote against the Lévesque referendum on separation, sovereignty or whatever, should be allowed to remain in Canada. Montreal businessman Lionel Albert, also a Union Nationale supporter, described the scheme as a "last resort", the idea being to create a new province from sections of Quebec which "wish to live without fear of separation from the rest of Canada."

Dr. Shaw had been telling his cohorts of "a week of tension" in Quebec City, with "intimidating" talk about having business conducted in French within five years, and the phasing out of English language schools within fifteen years. He was just trying to mobilize attitudes, he said. "Some people have told me it's dangerous to mobilize the English. But it's dangerous if we don't. If we don't exert democratic pressure we risk having some people become so frustrated that they'll resort to violence."

The committee, of course, abhors violence in the hypothetical, bilingual province of West Quebec. Anyway, Dr. Shaw told a meeting of 150 supporters that night, "I don't think for a minute that the referendum will ever pass. But we do have to be ready with a posture on concrete alternatives for the referendum, rather than abstract philosophies." By now Dr. Shaw was being identified in press reports as a man "who is not a member of the committee, but who has given it considerable support."

A month later the committee drew more than 1,000 people to a meeting. "This is not simply a preparatory committee for an eleventh province," non-member Shaw told the crowd. "It is saying to Mr. Lévesque: 'Well, if you can separate, so can we.' " They raised $3,000 that night, and claimed 1,200 members.

By early June the language was getting tougher. Lionel Albert, the former computer expert and committee chairman, said, according to an article in the *Westmount Examiner*, that any concessions to the Quebec government would simply "drive everything English, everything associated with the English, right out," along with "perhaps three million people." He mentioned concessions made to the Germans by Neville Chamberlain in 1938 and said that an "appeasement policy" might produce similar results leading to power for even more radical groups [than the Péquistes, presumably] for whom "racism and hatred . . . are meat and drink."

The *Westmount Examiner* was quick to point out that there were "scant numbers" of Westmount residents attending the meeting, which was held at Victoria Hall.

Meanwhile — Lord, how I wish I'd been present at that meeting — during this same post-election period, other grassroots anti-Péquiste groups were forming. Quebec Canada was founded by Liberal MNA Michel Gratton of Gatineau. Liberal MNA George Springate, of Westmount, founded Team Canada and the group later merged with Quebec Canada, which was claiming more than 15,000 members with "another 50,000 membership cards in circulation." Quebec Canada was planning a membership drive to collect 150,000 people by the end of 1977 which, if successful, would mean they'd outnumber the Parti Québécois.

If all of this seems confusing I'm not surprised, but it began to fall into place for me when, last October, I read an article by Richard Cleroux in the Toronto *Globe and Mail*. Cleroux omitted any reference to the Eleventh Province group but listed five grassroots organizations as "moving closer together, preparing to engage the Parti Québécois in what is shaping up as the greatest democratically fought battle in Quebec's history. Quebec's very future within Confederation is in the balance."

Later he described it as "a formidable challenge, a great

political undertaking no less significant than the formation of the Parti Québécois in 1968.''

Included were Quebec Canada, now claiming 150,000 members; the Council for Canadian Unity, a small but powerful organization of businessmen representing 150 of the wealthiest corporations in the country; the Positive Action Committee, a group of largely English-speaking Montrealers from the professions and universities; and two smaller groups, Decision Canada and Ralli-Canada.

The importance, wrote Cleroux, lay in the fact that while each of the groups had different visions of what the new Canada should be "they've agreed to keep their views to themselves for the time being, so as not to jeopardize their chances of beating the strongly united Parti Québécois forces in the referendum.''

Public opinion polls were showing that the Lévesque Government's popularity had risen, and, Cleroux wrote, "It has suddenly dawned on the province's federalists that unless they get together and do something, the referendum will be a walk-away win for the PQ.''

I know nothing further about the Eleventh Province group, nor am I much interested. Innuendoes of Naziism and racism can only worsen an already dangerously polarized situation. But the other groups may well achieve what the rest of Canada cannot. The referendum is not yet a battle between René Lévesque and Prime Minister Trudeau; it is a power struggle within the province of Quebec, with federal politicians on the defensive, capable only of sabre rattling and spending vast sums of money on national unity conferences across the land — generally a matter of preaching to the converted. That could change by the time these words appear in print but I still think the most satisfying and longlasting solution must come from within Quebec, and not from Ottawa. Ottawa can certainly contribute and someday may begin (although I see no intelligent moves emanating from that insular city as yet) but if Canada is to survive it must be because Canadians want it to survive. Particularly those Canadians of French persuasion.

I WAS INTERESTED in learning about the misguided Eleventh Province group because it led me to the other, responsible groups who are fighting my battle for me in Quebec, burying their philosophical differences to form a coalition against a common threat. The Toronto newspapers have devoted enormous chunks of space to the question of national unity but mostly this comes in the form of think-pieces written by academics and other intellectuals, as well as massive coverage of essentially boring and irrelevant national unity conferences. Only a handful of writers like Cleroux consistently report on Quebec politics as such. Or so it seems to me.

I left my friends about ten o'clock that night to catch an eleven o'clock bus for Quebec City. I'd picked up a copy of *Maclean's Magazine* and was reading Allan Fotheringham's column and suddenly I found — not terribly surprisingly — that he, too, had considered the elitism of the Lévesque cabinet, as had my luncheon companion the day before. And of course he'd done his homework, which is partly why his columns can be so devastating. He wrote:

One of the factors of the PQ that English Canada does not understand is that one of the reasons why its leaders have so little commitment to Canada is that they have little interest or background in Canada. Their ideas have been shaped outside this country.

Education Minister Jacques-Yvan Morin studied at Harvard and Cambridge, taught at the University of Paris and was a member of the International Court at The Hague. Finance Minister Jacques Parizeau is a product of the London School of Economics and Paris. Dr. [Camille] Laurin studied in Boston, spent four years in Paris and was with the world university interaid in Geneva. Claude Morin, of Intergovernmental Affairs, is a Columbia man. Denis Lazure, of Social Affairs, is a U. of Pennsylvania product. Natural Resources minister Yves Berube is from M.I.T. Pierre Marois of Social Development is from the Sorbonne. Denis de Belleval, in charge of public service, studied in Britain and Germany. The labor minister, Jacques Couture speaks Chinese. The communications minister, Louis O'Neill, studied theology in Rome. These really are the best and brightest. Lévesque has a thorough international background from war and broadcasting.

AND THERE'S an ex-naval commander in Perth, Ontario, who thinks *Trudeau* is conspiring to transform Canada into a French nation! The mind boggles. He's sold sixty thousand books in Canada. Does that mean there are sixty thousand Canadians who *believe* him?

THE BUS PULLED into Quebec City at 1:45 a.m., Saturday, June 11. I was far too keyed up to consider going to bed. I was staying at the Victoria Hotel, a far cry from comfort anyway. Everything was closed, except for a disco and it, too, would close soon. I gritted my teeth, paid my dollar membership and strolled in, blinking, blinded by a thousand mirrors multiplying the merciless strobelights.

And that is how I met two girls from Matane. And discovered that even when you combine language and politics, there needn't be a barrier.

I was trying to figure out what sort of place I'd walked into but I couldn't see a pattern. Few people were dancing; mostly they were sitting around talking. The women were attractively dressed but there was no sign of a prostitute's overdone makeup, no sign of anyone obviously gay. Two pleasant girls were giggling about something and one of them came over to me, blushing, and said "My friend says you are veree 'andsome" and then she fled.

Now, I didn't know what to make of that. After nearly three hours on the bus, I wasn't feeling "veree 'andsome". But clearly some response was called for, and just as clearly the pair lacked the hardness of streetwalkers. They just looked . . . nice. I approached the one who'd spoken to me and said "Votre amie est tres jolie, aussi." Then I returned to my position, leaning back against the bar. More giggling and the first girl approached again. "You may join us, if you like," she said, then turned rapidly — to cover embarrassment? — and rejoined her friend.

I pondered. They both looked about eighteen or nineteen years old, no more; unsophisticated but friendly, that much was clear. What did they want of me? The mini-bars were scattered about the place, just counters, about chest high. It was the strangest come-on I'd ever encountered, all preliminaries conducted by an intermediary, not the slightest hint of flirtation: an invitation. To what, I didn't know.

The first girl turned to me. "My friend doesn't speak English very well," she said.

Useless small talk. Do you come here often? I began to comprehend: they wanted nothing from me. They'd seen that I was alone, perhaps lonely; that I looked interesting and so they invited me to join them, nothing more. I learned that they were from Matane, a small community on the Gaspé peninsula, office girls or salesgirls. They'd come to Quebec City for a few days' vacation but were returning to work early next morning. Early *this* morning. The first girl went to the powder room and I spoke with her friend, explaining as best I could, what I was doing, and why. I showed her the little map I carried, showing all the various bus routes with my own progress marked in brown Pentel. She seemed to understand and said something about René Lévesque being a good man.

"Vous êtes separatiste?" I asked.

She shrugged. "Il est un bon homme."

"Vous n'aimez pas les anglais?"

She turned and smiled. "It is not that," she said, speaking English for the first time. "It is our destiny."

"C'est une destinée tragique pour tout le monde," I said. She shrugged, but it was a friendly shrug. Her friend returned and the two chattered rapidly together for a moment, and then she turned to me.

"Would you like to drive to Matane with us?" she asked.

"Thank you," I said, "but I have a bus schedule. My bus leaves at four o'clock."

"You could take the train from Matane to Campbellton (New Brunswick) and meet the bus there."

"Thank you, but I must stay with my schedule," I said. "And you are leaving so early. I need to sleep. *Je suis très fatigué.* " She nodded. The bar was closed now, so we parted and as I walked back to my hotel I wondered if I'd missed an opportunity. We would have driven to Matane, talking along the way. One or other of the two would have taken me to her parents' home or farm and I might have learned much. Pity.

There was more to it than that, of course, but I had made the wrong choice. My Montreal friend had arranged with the bureau chief of his newspaper for me to sit in on the Bill One hearings for a while that day, sometime after lunch.

It had seemed a good idea, and it was this, largely, that had dissuaded me from going to Matane. But the bureau people never turned up and I did not get into the red room of the Quebec National Assembly.

At about three o'clock I approached a policeman, asking if he could tell me where the bus terminal was. He could indeed and did so, at great length. As I followed his instructions, I realized he had been totally wrong; I was heading away from the bus terminal; I could feel it in my bones. I hailed a cab and he proved me right, getting me there just in time to board the four o'clock bus to Edmundston, New Brunswick.

THE MARITIMES
If Norway can do it . . .

A YOUTH IN his late teens approached me in the bus depot at Edmundston the next morning, tanned and muscular but with the dead-eyed gaze of the panhandler. He was looking for work, he said, and his unemployment insurance money was gone until the next payment, later on in the week. He was hungry.

"Is it so difficult to get a job?" I asked. "Are things as bad in New Brunswick as they're supposed to be?" He just looked at me, silently, wondering, perhaps, whether I would give him money or a lecture. I gave him just over a dollar in change and he started away with not even a nod of appreciation. I tried to hold his attention with some comment or question which I've forgotten, and he paused briefly.

"I haven't eaten since yesterday morning," he said.

He left and for a moment or two I felt both annoyed and chagrined. Annoyed by the defeated expression on his face, chagrined by my own intrusiveness. I needn't have worried, I think. He did not automatically head for a nearby restaurant. He systematically approached other travelers. What bothered me most, I think, was that he just didn't look very hungry and I felt used. Hard to be sure one way or the other.

I boarded the bus to endure the four-and-a-half hour run to Fredericton, and I do mean *endure*. The buses I rode through New Brunswick were the worst I encountered in the entire country, the drivers just short of being openly rude. Not an auspicious beginning to the final segment of my journey and I began to feel a sense of foreboding.

I whiled away the hours watching the Saint John River flowing beside the narrow highway, wondering why there wasn't any boating on it. I never did find out. Aside from that there was little to see but pine forests and the many hamlets and towns we stopped at; it was a real milk run, which explains why it took nearly five hours to travel 178 miles. Eventually we arrived at Fredericton and I checked in at the Lord Beaverbrook Hotel, then gathered all my clothing and headed for a laundromat about six blocks away. I forgot to take any reading material with me and it was drizzling outside, humid and crowded inside and I sat on the wooden steps of the building listening somewhat gloomily to the desultory conversation of the people waiting, like myself, for the cycles to end. There was a young couple lounging against the railing and smoking. Both were clad in denim and they were an attractive pair, exuding an air of if not prosperity at least confidence. But they didn't speak, they waited mindlessly and reminded me of the look you often see on the faces of people in an elevator. It's dead time and you simply close down your mind.

I was trying not to make judgments, not to characterize an entire province by the listless appearance of a handful of people and I wasn't being very successful. I have been in New Brunswick four or five times in the last six or seven years and have felt this way before. It's such a pretty place, and people often seem deeply rooted, immovably so, but sometimes I wonder if they enjoy it. Not that they're unfriendly — it's just a general absence of enthusiasm.

Later I asked a friend in Toronto, who lived for several

years in New Brunswick and whose wife was born there, about this apparent listlessness and he put it into a more positive perspective. The province is very poor, he said, and in many ways mediocre. "But the people are jewels and it's a very enjoyable place to live. However, you can't farm and there aren't any minerals and the fishing isn't supported or organized. They're doing all right in lobster and shellfish but they'd have to go the route of Japan and Russia to develop fishing, investing in ships and equipment.

"You can't do anything industrially in New Brunswick because there's no skilled labor force, it's too far from markets and there aren't the resources. Kids graduating from trade schools pretty well have to leave the province to find jobs.

"One of the problems is that the people haven't been exposed to the entrepreneurship that there is in central Canada, they've never seen that kind of go-ahead attitude. My brother-in-law works in the post office in Fredericton and he plays baseball and hockey and he's never even been to Nova Scotia. There are a lot of people like that with absolutely no desire to travel."

EVENTUALLY MY clothes were clean and dry. I folded them and called a cab — it was raining heavily now — and after a long time one came by; I waved at it frantically and it stopped. It was the company I had called, all right, but clearly no one had been dispatched to collect me.

The driver deposited me back at the hotel. I tried to draw him into conversation and he grunted pleasantly enough but wouldn't rise to the bait. I went to my room and worked for a while, typing notes and scribbling down random observations before I went down to the lobby to find some lunch and perhaps someone to talk to. The weather was so filthy that I decided to stay in the hotel, except for a brief excursion to the Beaverbrook Art Gallery next door. Although I'd visited Fredericton several times I'd never seen it. It didn't take long. I've never been high on Cornelius Krieghoff and the huge Salvador Dali is so cluttered up with symbolism that after a long glance I decided to hell with it, and went back to the hotel.

There was a meeting of economists in the hotel, part of the Conference of Learned Societies. I met a few of them but we had little common ground. Theirs is an arcane field with a lousy track record. I was more interested in a pharmacist in the lounge who explained to me at great length that [a] he was *not* drunk, and [b] his wife was working and *not* running around and [c] that even if she was he was beating her at that game anyway. He disapproved of many things, had a job he hated, a wife he didn't trust and a three-bedroom bungalow which he bought five years before for $34,000. Today it had to be worth $60,000 but it was paper profit; it would cost him much more than that to find a better home because of inflation. It seemed almost deliberate: his abject wallowing in self-pity mocked my gloom and I left him shortly feeling almost euphoric in contrast, bent on finding the best steak in town. That, the desk clerk assured me, would be in the hotel's restaurant and since it was still raining heavily I decided to believe him, and wasn't disappointed. It was a good dinner.

Back to my room. I'd sworn to do some work that night and I had some tapes to transcribe, but my tape recorder decided it was a radio, picking up music and commercials as well as the fluorescent lighting so I gave it up and spent the evening listening to the entertainment in the lounge, chatting idly with various people and learning little.

I checked out of the hotel late next morning and went to the bus depot to check the schedule for Moncton. I had been hoping to visit Leonard Jones, one-time mayor of Moncton, now a Member of Parliament. I'd done an article about him a year or so before, after Robert Stanfield kicked him out of the Progressive Conservative caucus because of Jones' antagonism toward New Brunswick's Acadians. I wondered if he'd still be speaking to me — it wasn't a friendly article. There was still a half hour before the bus would leave so I sat on a bench and relaxed.

Two old men were there, one dressed in a suit which had seen better days, the other jacketless, with suspenders, a shirt left open at the neck and, so help me, a straw boater. They were passing the time of day and I tuned in idly. They were talking about another man who had died recently and the man in the suit was asking if the fellow had been wealthy. He'd heard that he was.

Straw hat and suspenders got kind of excited about that. "Money!" he snorted. "That's all anybody thinks about, *money*. If you haven't got it you're a nobody. All I need is three meals a day and a place to sleep. That's all anybody needs."

The man in the suit mumbled something I didn't catch. Straw hat and suspenders made his final judgment: "Well," he said, "he may have been a millionaire but he's the same as a poor man now."

The bus arrived and I boarded it, stowing my bags in the overhead rack without thinking. I was trying to figure out why straw hat and suspenders' comment had disturbed me and the word that came to mind was "passive". On the prairies, in the far west and certainly in the much-detested central part of Canada there's an aggressiveness toward life. You work, you strive, depending on your dreams and aspirations, and here was a Maritimer scoffing at the rat race. A man old enough to have had to struggle through the depression, maybe support a family and he just didn't give a damn. This was New Brunswick, one of the founding provinces of Confederation, definitely a have-not province with a population of about 600,000. Hardly enough for a decent city. Backyard swings and stately elms and peeling paint — oh, that may be unfair and I was only passing through. But that was what I was feeling, and it was reflected in the ambience of the town, the surliness of the driver, the indignation of the couple sitting across the aisle from me. They'd been complaining to the driver that they were hungry and he'd just turned his back on them. I asked where they were from, where they were headed. Nice, middle-aged couple from Thunder Bay where the man works at a grain elevator. They had two weeks vacation and had left the previous Friday night, travelling non-stop to Amherst to visit family there. They'd been going all the time; the whole journey would take approximately two and a half days and they hadn't had a decent meal since they'd left. The driver should stop for meal breaks at decent restaurants, surely? I said he should indeed, adding that I hadn't had bad luck until I hit New Brunswick. Elsewhere the lunch and dinner stops weren't exactly *haute cuisine* but by and large they'd been adequate.

Soon the driver stopped, announcing a lunch break. The restaurant was closed. There was a coffee machine and a bubble gum dispenser and that's all, I swear it.

At this point, I decided I wasn't feeling much like talking to people so I'd push on to Saint John, and if I didn't feel like stopping there I'd bloody well stay put until we got to Halifax. I knew the symptoms: I was beginning to deteriorate physically, emotionally, psychologically, *journalistically*. I'd been on the road just short of a month and I'd traveled more than 4,000 miles.

A friend of mine once asked me how I make contact with people on such an expedition. "Well," I said, "you know me as a fairly intense, serious-minded guy." He nodded. "Well, when I'm away on an assignment, often, if conditions are right, I can shed my inhibitions, drop my distancing mechanisms and open up to people. I become both participant and observer, absorbing what I can, digesting and considering. My whole personality changes and I don't put people off the way I tend to do at home. The last thing you want on a crowded subway is contact with your fellow sardines. When you're traveling it's different."

It's true but there are limits. After a while a craving for privacy develops, up go the barriers and I withdraw into myself.

Actually I was lucky that day. I met an old friend, an Ottawa-based television producer I'd known in Washington, and we chatted as far as Saint John, where he was visiting a sister. He'd been one of the speakers at the Fredericton conference but I hadn't seen him until shortly before we boarded the same bus. I also met a woman who'd been part of the conference and the three of us talked idly.

Before he left us, my television friend — who has an eclectic mind — observed that Saint John is redemption city in Canada. "It's true," he said, "whenever you look at the address on grocery coupons (ten cents off on a bottle of instant coffee) it's always in Saint John. He also asked why Prince Edward Island potatoes cost twice as much as New Brunswick potatoes and I don't know the answer to that one, either. There was a brief lunch stop and when I came back to the bus, trying not to spill a paper cup brim full of black coffee, I found I'd made my decision. The House was sitting in Ottawa and Leonard Jones, MP, would not likely be home so I opted for the ten-hour run from Fredericton to Saint John to Moncton to Halifax. It would be a long, uncomfortable haul but a time when I could either be by myself or talk: a time to try to loosen up.

About a third of New Brunswick's people are Acadians whose historical roots go back to 1604 when the first French colony was established there. They are French Canadians with as strong a claim to Canada as their cousins in Quebec and while most of them are bilingual, they still think of themselves as French. They're concentrated in the northern counties, along the Quebec border to the west, and down the coast of the Gulf of St. Lawrence to Northumberland Strait.

When I visited Moncton to do the article on Leonard Jones, I spoke with Claude Borque, editor of the French language newspaper *L'Evangeline*, local newspaper reporters and people in the street. All of them agreed — even Borque, as I recall — that ninety-five per cent of the Acadians *do* speak English. They are more or less integrated but they do not want to be assimilated. There has been much friction between French and English and Jones, while Mayor, was implacably opposed to recognizing their cultural aspirations which led to some ugly incidents. Moncton built its first French language high school in the early 1960s. In Saint John, the province's largest city, there are close to seven thousand people whose mother tongue is French but until 1977 there hadn't been French classes for them and even then only grade one classes were made available.

For many years there was an uneasy truce in the province.

But as the quiet revolution occurred in Quebec it reverberated in Acadia and now, with René Lévesque warning that the only place in Canada for French Canadians is Quebec, they feel increasingly isolated, increasingly threatened. Certainly there's no question that New Brunswick is dominated by the English. They came and conquered two hundred years ago, creating a volatile mixture of English Protestants and French Catholics. Loyalists and New Englanders were followed by Irish immigrants as a result of the potato famine. But the Acadians were there first. Changes are taking place but slowly. Late in the summer of 1977 a bilingual reporter tried to check into one of Moncton's major hotels, speaking French. The man behind the desk, according to one report, "angrily interrupted" saying, "I can't understand a word you're saying. You'll have to come back in an hour and there'll be someone who can understand you."

Which sounds a little more promising than a few years ago, when Mayor Leonard Jones refused to permit Dr. Michael Cripton to speak a few words of French during a council meeting. Cripton had led the polls in a vote for alderman-at-large and, in fact, had outpolled the mayor himself. Jones, whose supporters were jeering Cripton, told him to "confine yourself to something we can all understand."

I asked Leonard Jones about the incident and he said "if I hadn't done that, if I'd let him speak French, there would have been a riot."

How a politician can ignore the aspirations of thirty-five per cent of his constituents is beyond me.

W E ARRIVED in Halifax about ten o'clock; I checked into the Lord Nelson Hotel and went to the restaurant. Since it was closed, I went through to the Trafalgar Lounge to enquire about a restaurant that might be open and that is where I met Harry the super salesman, a Newfie who lives in Toronto but who spends most of his time roaming the Maritimes selling auto parts. Harry is irrepressible and he'd just visited one of his clients, expecting an order for several hundred dollars and getting instead an order for $4,000. He was a problem to me. He wanted to celebrate but you can't celebrate alone and so he elected me. I wanted to eat and go to bed so we compromised by going to a restaurant for a late dinner.

Harry was appalled when I told him what I had done — traveled from Victoria to Halifax by bus, but when he learned I intended to continue north to Sydney, take the ferry to Port aux Basques and cross Newfoundland by bus as well he began to treat me like a retarded child. "For God's sake, John," he said, his face contorted with concern, "take the plane. Fly to St. John's. Fly home. That's boonie-land, take my advice and don't do it."

And then, of course, he began to tell me about Newfoundland, where to stay, who to see. "Corner Brook is beautiful," he said. "Stay at the Glyn Mill Inn. You'll really like it. I got a cousin in Corner Brook, he's the city clerk. And when you get to St. John's stay at the Hotel Newfoundland. Maybe I'll see you there; I've gotta see some clients in Newfie. You know there's 500,000 people in Newfoundland and there's 500,000 lakes. And St. John's is the only city in North America where the cops don't wear guns. And the bars! When it's closing time the bartender just locks the door and says 'Now, me sons, let's get down to some serious drinking'."

"But you gotta remember you're in real frontier country there," he said. "The cuisine isn't the best."

Eventually I disentangled myself from Harry and went to bed. I couldn't figure him out at all. He obviously loved his island but he couldn't comprehend my wanting to go there. Not at all. Nor could he stop talking about it. Ah well, it takes all types.

I wasn't able to visit Prince Edward Island; there simply wasn't time. It was a disappointment, too, because I spent a couple of summers there when I was young. Recently the federal task force on unity convened in Charlottetown and Premier Alex Campbell wanted to "reconvene the meeting of the fathers of Confederation so that we may revive our discussions on the subject of national unity and the means of achieving it." The issue, he felt, "is Quebec. We are here because of the possibility that six million Canadians may leave Canada." Two hundred and fifty people attended the session, but according to one report I read, "Many of the speakers didn't even mention the threat to Canadian unity posed by Quebec's separatist Parti Québécois government. They complained instead about the economic domination of 'Central Canada,' especially Ontario."

Shortly after I returned home I read another report from Charlottetown pointing out — and this astonished me — that roughly one-seventh of the 119,000 Islanders are Acadians. A report prepared by the St. Thomas Aquinas Society for the Federation of Francophones Outside Quebec chided the government for its failure to provide cultural facilities for the minority, and warned that the Island's Acadians had remained acquiescent and accommodating for far too long. The Society planned to adopt a more aggressive stance, and to encourage Acadians to press for changes within the educational system. Fine. It's the squeaking wheel that gets the oil. Politicians rarely move until they're pushed and a fourteen per cent minority shouldn't have much trouble gaining concessions from an essentially benign government.

What I did hear throughout the Atlantic provinces was a combination of apprehension and resentment, much the same as I'd heard in the West. Richard Gwyn, syndicated Ottawa columnist, touched on this when he reviewed a book called *Canada and the Burden of Unity*, a collection of essays written by various regional academics. "The entire volume," wrote Gwyn, "is about how the burden of national unity is being carried by the bookends of Confederation, the four western provinces and the four Atlantic ones, all for the benefit of Ontario and Quebec, snug in the centre."

He also quoted Nova Scotia provincial NDP member Paul McEwan, author of *Confederation and the Maritimes* as saying "In the next few years, Maritimers are going to be giving Confederation one last chance . . . . [We] are bone-weary of paying through the nose to support our fat and parasitic brethren in the Montreal-Sarnia fertile crescent."

On my first day in Halifax I went to see James D. McNiven,

executive vice-president of the Atlantic Provinces Economic Council. Jim McNiven is actually a native of Michigan, although his father was a Manitoban. He's an economist, with degrees from the University of Winnipeg and the University of Michigan and taught at Western and Dalhousie. He described the Canadian malaise as being "like a party that's sort of dull and everybody would like to go home but nobody makes the first move . . . I get the feeling that part of the country is perfectly content. It's not even Ontario; you draw a line from Parry Sound to Ottawa.

"It's a funny thing. You find all kinds of little movements all over the country. A couple of years ago the mayors and municipalities of Cape Breton signed a proposal asking Ottawa to reconsider establishing Cape Breton as a separate province, because it used to be a colony until 1826, when it was absorbed by Nova Scotia. And you find movements in places like Labrador and in parts of Quebec . . . . If there's anything distinctive about Canadians it's their ability to divide themselves into ever smaller groups."

"We hear Anglophones from Ontario and Montreal saying 'If Quebec gives us too much trouble we'll just put up a big barrier, a Berlin Wall so to speak,' and people down here say 'Wait a minute, we're on the other side of that thing too. What's going to happen to us?' and nobody hears this because they're so busy shouting, like two parents shouting at each other and not hearing the kids say 'What about us?'

"There's a real fear that if this thing really gets bad, this area is just going to be allowed to float on its own . . . . This has caused an awful lot of concern. This whole region has about two million people; Quebec has *six* million people.

"So all right, there's a fear here. There's an aggressive Quebec pushing on the Atlantic region and the problem with Labrador — you know, Quebec never really accepted the British Privy Council decision in 1928 [turning Labrador over to the Newfoundlanders]. It didn't really matter until they started realizing the hydro potential. So this business of talking about the Acadians possibly forming their own province, all it does is tell a lot of people down here that this is what we can expect: pushing and pushing and pushing. We're not talking about within Confederation or out, it doesn't make any difference. In this area there are going to be some vast changes and I don't think people realize that. Cultural changes."

I asked him if he saw Quebec as an economic threat.

"Oh sure," he said, "there have been things happening already. A lot of our smaller communities used to depend on the *caisse populaires* in Quebec as a market for municipal bonds. Now the Quebec Government wants the *caisse populaires* to start buying more Quebec municipal bonds. These municipalities are too small to go to the Toronto markets, or New York. Quebec is saying 'let's buy our own' and suddenly the Nova Scotia municipalities have trouble selling their bonds."

He turned to unemployment saying "It's very hard to take a blanket look at it, and this is what Ottawa tends to do. Labrador has a population of 32,000. Eastern Labrador, Goose Bay — that's a real disaster area right now. In western Labrador the iron mines are doing all right. But Ottawa melds them together, along with Newfoundland and Prince Edward Island. The estimates I had of the eastern side of Prince Edward Island, in the winter, were on the order of something like fifty-five per cent unemployment. It can be really grim, and you go ten miles down the road and things will be all right . . . . To be honest with you, Ottawa, for all its talk, just doesn't give a damn."

In other words — and any cub reporter learns in his first three months how bureaucrats and politicians can lie with statistics — if you take a street with ten families and examine their situation you might find nine of them are thriving and the tenth is starving. So you take the average per-family income and on paper it will look like a fairly prosperous street. That doesn't mean the tenth family isn't going hungry. It often does mean that politically that family doesn't exist.

"Sydney, for example, in Cape Breton," he continued. "The mines are at a low output so you've got maybe twenty, twenty-two per cent unemployment there. Halifax isn't doing too badly. In Newfoundland, Corner Brook is fairly prosperous but in a place like Buchans, the mine's going to close down in a couple of years and the town is going to die."

Bitter words. But then he changes gear and tells me that "the economic arguments for or against Confederation are simply a red herring. Totally irrelevant. The real thing is do you want to live with your neighbors or don't you? Canada for so long has had the luxury of saying [about other Canadians in distant parts of the country] well, they're so far away that I can bitch about them and not have to worry. Now we're forced to make a decision. What's happened has brought the country closer together, you're more aware of the animosities." And that is the problem of the television generation, the global village. It's an irony.

"You know," he said, "in a sense the United States is regarded with less hostility here than Upper Canada. There's always been a feeling that we ought to join the States. My own feeling is that the Americans don't need four more West Virginias. And they don't want to have to start worrying about their neighbors. It would be a nuisance to have to be bothered with a Canada that's falling apart."

Transportation?

"You see, the government is working against us. They went over to a kind of transportation policy which they call a user-pay system. Now it's user-pay except for things like the St. Lawrence Seaway. Everywhere else you pay. This translates into southern Ontario getting the goodies and everyone else getting shafted."

Transportation probably causes more headaches in Canada than anything else. Building the St. Lawrence Seaway, for example, was in itself an act of Central Canadian economic imperialism. It virtually destroyed Halifax as a major port.

The federal government decided, about a year and a half ago, to write off the $842 million debt still outstanding from seaway construction. After seventeen years the seaway still hadn't paid for itself and clearly wasn't going to.

When it was a-building we thought it would transform our lives. Ships would penetrate far into the interior and prices of imported goods would plummet! In Toronto we were titillated by the appearance of Russian freighters. But there were no economic miracles after all. Except for obliterating the port of Halifax.

From the Atlantic provinces the view of Ottawa was black indeed. Who had built the seaway? Ottawa. Who covered its operating losses? Ottawa. Who kept it open in the winter with expensive ice-breakers? Ottawa. Who did the seaway help? Ontario. Who did it hurt? Nova Scotia.

One critic observed that Ontario, by using the seaway, was able to import coal from Pennsylvania "at the same time that coal mines are being shut down in Nova Scotia. Not only that, it's paid a subsidy to do so."

We don't call it "eastern alienation" but it amounts to the same thing: Central Canada couldn't care less about eastern economic disasters. Confederation itself was designed to preserve the central economy, not to strengthen the nation as a whole.

I TALKED WITH Jim McNiven for a while and left, walking back to the hotel and thinking.

If all the people I'd been listening to for the past month were right, then Ottawa — parliament, bureaucracy, senate and all — is corrupt, never mind which party happens to be in power, since it's been going on for 110 years. If all the people were wrong, then Trudeau must be right to call us a nation of whiners. But how can so many people, from so many parts of the country, all be wrong? Especially when the arguments they use are so similar? And if "Central Canada" means Ontario *and* Quebec, why does Quebec want out? Is René Lévesque simply indulging in emotional blackmail, playing on regional apprehensions to improve the lot of Quebeckers? Too many dismal questions.

The sun was shining and felt good so I went through the ornate iron gates of Springbank Garden, across the road from the hotel, and sat on a bench watching the world pass by. I didn't want to think, I wanted to empty my mind for awhile and after an hour or so I had a light dinner and hailed a cab. I'd invited myself over to John MacCormack's home for the evening and I put a fresh cassette in my tape recorder. I didn't feel like taking notes and I don't trust my memory; it leaks.

John MacCormack is Professor of History and Director (as well as founder) of the Institute of Human Values at Saint Mary's University in Halifax. I'd met him the previous autumn when the institute held a seminar, and then I read an article he'd written on "The Canadian Crisis", which was excerpted in the *Toronto Star*.

"We have a constitution," he had written, "that is the result of a forced marriage between parliamentary absolutism and federalism. It produces a situation in which constitutional amendments are subject to party politics, personal confrontations and bargains struck between heads of governments, and in which the Bill of Rights is of doubtful force and permanence . . . . If English-speaking Canadians are to understand the Québécois they must remember that for two centuries they have lived with a sense of being unfree and that their sharing in the Canadian story has not been without a continuing element of duress . . . . Need we be surprised that out of this emerged a demand for complete national sovereignty for Quebec? It would have been more surprising if no such movement had developed . . . .

"René Lévesque has a vision of an independent Quebec. It is based on a 19th century concept of ethnic and linguistic nationalism but it retains a powerful appeal for a people whose memories are long. It can be countered only by calling on the people of Canada to engage in a great collective enterprise: no less than the refounding of this nation on a basis of true federalism, a nation open to 20th century multiculturalism and dedicated to the pursuit of justice and freedom."

I asked him to expand on this and he told me "I think we should work out a constitution that would be flexible, that is to say if a province wanted to take more power for itself it could — within limits, of course — or it could take less. In other words Quebec could take quite a bit more and the other provinces could take less. Instead of *giving* to Quebec as a special case, allow it to be open-ended so that other provinces could take similar powers if they wanted to. It's risky, but I don't like the idea of special status. When you work out a constitution it should be the same for everybody, but providing for different situations.''

MacCormack had already made it clear that he felt the constitution is inadequate and presumably that Confederation isn't working, and I raised two questions (reminding myself of his Nova Scotian chauvinism). One was a description of my vague unease in New Brunswick, and the feeling I'd had when the bus crossed into Nova Scotia that a burden had been lifted from my shoulders or psyche. Could he account for that? I told him of the contempt I'd sensed on the prairies — contempt for a perceived, passive acceptance in the Maritimes. Mid-westerners I'd talked with were aggressive when they talked of Confederation, and wondered why Maritimers weren't the same. After all, many of their arguments, their grievances are similar.

"Nova Scotia," he said, "is a much happier province than New Brunswick. New Brunswick is the Loyalist province. The Loyalists made a great contribution to Canada, there's no doubt about that, but of course they carried with them a lot of attitudes. A lot of them didn't go through the pioneering process and they were in many cases bitterly anti-American, pro-British. Their affirmation of their British roots was exaggerated, as it was in southern Ontario. They were also anti-Catholic, many of them, and there were a lot of French people in the regions where they landed. It was a sort of ethnic-cultural-religious thing.

"The Indians and the French were often in alliance but the New Englanders never got along with the Indians and of course they accused the French of setting the Indians on them, which they may have done.''

So much for the historical setting. "You can't understand Saint John without understanding Rothesay, which is a suburb of Saint John and one of the most self-confident areas in Canada. They're vigorous and nice people with the feeling that they were born to rule, that they run New Brunswick, *which is now over fifty per cent Catholic*, and about thirty per cent

French. The only province in Canada that is [outside of Quebec]."

I felt I was beginning to understand, despite the tactfully indirect response. New Brunswickers were a mixture of conquered, spiteful French; bitterly anti-American Loyalists and starved Irish potato farmers. It couldn't have been easy. "The idea that the French would ever get uppity was just sort of ruled out completely." Nova Scotia, as the name implies, was largely settled by the Scots highlanders, rough-hewn people who didn't like to be pushed around. Nova Scotia became more democratic.

We switched to the matter of western contempt and for the first time MacCormack sounded almost bitter. Defensive.

"There's been a real deterioration of the self-image of the Maritimes," he said. "It's been accentuated by television. If you go back to the 1870s the self-image of Nova Scotians was clear-cut and self-confident. Nova Scotia was fourth in world merchant shipping tonnage. There were Nova Scotian ships in ports all over the world. It was a prosperous time. The factors in decline? Two world wars cost the province a loss of leadership, relatively more than other parts of Canada. And then there was the economic decline from Confederation down to about fifteen years ago. It's said to be reversing now.

"Even in the thirties, when I was born, we still felt Nova Scotia did things better than anywhere else. I think the main thing wrong with Nova Scotia right now is the deterioration of that self-image. Everybody who comes here likes it, admires it and so on but Nova Scotians have started to feel that somehow or other we're a backwater.

"Television is controlled by Toronto as far as English-speaking Canada is concerned, as far as the image of the Maritimes is concerned. Disparaging wisecracks hurt. They may seem unimportant on the surface but if that kind of image is transmitted to us, that we're backward, the equivalent of Canada's south, that we're ignorant, stupid — everything we always thought we weren't — this starts to get to people after a while. They start to accept it."

The global village again. In the old days you could say what you wanted secure in the knowledge that Quebeckers, Westerners, Easterners would never hear about it. "Now we're getting this feedback and we hear about immigrants from the Maritimes, welfare cases and so on. It's annoying and humiliating."

And what about Maritime separatism? "Well a change has taken place in the last fifteen years and I'm not sure what the political implications are. I'd say it's potential, there's political dynamite there . . . a growing sense of determination to find out what the Maritimes are all about, what we've got going here. The right person wouldn't have too much difficulty generating quite a strong separatist movement here. We've gone through a low point of despair.

"The main grievance of the Atlantic area is the feeling that we're not appreciated by the rest of the country. The tariff structure is designed to favor Central Canada. For example, we export frozen fish blocks to the States because the Americans structure their tariff policy so they do all the manufacturing. So this results in us exporting frozen fish blocks which are converted into fish sticks in the United States and exported back to Canada . . .

"We had a coal problem here. The Gordon Report said 'phase out the coal mines.' At that time Ontario Hydro was just about the best customer for Pennsylvania coal. If we said why not import ours, they said don't be ridiculous, it's cheaper this way. But if we said it's cheaper to import radios or cars or television sets made in Pennsylvania, the argument didn't apply. In other words it's a national policy when it suits the interests of southern Ontario and it's a protectionist policy when it suits the interests of southern Ontario and either way we get it in the neck."

And it struck me: here's a Nova Scotian academic and he sounds just like a prairie farmer or a northern Ontario motel operator. And I thought, if you hear a thing often enough, and from enough people, sooner or later you're going to start believing it.

MacCormack returned to the coal mines. "Gordon came and wanted to shut down the coal mines. I said, if you do you won't be able to open them up again. You can't just take a man off the street in Toronto and send him into a coal mine . . ."

And the economics of separation? "I don't see why this area couldn't be economically viable. We'd go through a period when the loss of equalization payments would be serious. But possibly the psychological effect would be good. Equalization payments have helped the economy, but some people think it's income. What equalization payments have done is to provide us with good schools and roads but they don't do anything for the fisherman."

Next year they'll be reopening some of the mines. Ottawa has finally realized there's an energy crisis coming, and that Nova Scotia alone has some 190 million tons of recoverable coal. It's a dirty, difficult trade and coal is a notorious pollutant. Keeps you warm in the winter, though.

R ENTED A LITTLE car next morning. A friend wanted me to meet "the Major" — she thought I might find him interesting. I picked her up at her home in Dartmouth and we drove out into the countryside north of Dartmouth, along country roads until we came to a service station owned by her brother and his wife and we stopped for coffee and conversation. Then we all piled into his car — mine was just too small — and drove a quarter mile further, stopping at a century-old farm house. More coffee, more conversation. He isn't really a major and never was. His name is Albro Thompson and he's 81 years old; he and his wife just passed their diamond wedding anniversary and they had a nice letter from Prime Minister Trudeau. They liked that. They're true blue Tories. Stanfield and Diefenbaker Tories. Joe Clark was a disappointment, a mistake. "They'll never beat Trudeau with Clark."

The old man was adopted when he was four or five years old. Somebody called him "the Major" and the name stuck. The name lettered on the mail box is Major Albro Thompson" but nobody calls him "Albro" or "Mr. Thompson." He's a delightful old character, outspoken, blunt and hopelessly partisan. He's also lived a dozen lives. "I bought the farm in

1928," he told me. "I bought 124 acres. It had been a 1,000-acre farm at the start. Just grants of land. Just the farm and a bit of woodland." We were sitting in the parlor and the womenfolk were amusing themselves in the kitchen. Women's lib didn't touch his generation.

"As they lumbered the land I kept buying pieces of it and I got it all back except for 600 acres. I got 328 acres across the river in 1939 for $200. About the same time, in the early thirties, I had an opportunity to buy 250 acres for $100 but I didn't have the money. Bought it in 1955 for $2,000."

Eventually he had something like 1,400 acres of farmland and now, in his retirement, he's developing it. "It's not all sunshine, either. Surveying is expensive, cutting out the streets, developing it, and when I get it ready for sale the government takes 46 per cent. Why bother? Oh, I have to have something to do. I worked in landscaping until I was 80 and retired . . . ."

When he was sixty he had 50 head of cattle wiped out by Bang's Disease. Too expensive to start over again, so that's when he went into the landscaping business. And in 1941 there was a forest fire that burned all the land he had, right up to the house. "So I started to work as a carpenter, painter, working at the shipyards. I helped the electric welders, worked from the bottom of the ship to the top of the mast. Just a helper, I had no skills. I was in my 50s."

I was beginning to realize why they'd wanted me to meet the Major. He comes about as close as a living man can to the pioneer. You worked and saved and if things went badly you started over again. Grade nine education "which was a pretty good education in those days. I was carrying deal when I was 13. Makes a strong body." Deal was the old way they cut lumber.

"Quebec?" he repeated. The Major's hard of hearing and he'd repeat whatever I yelled at him and then he'd pause for a moment and start talking. "Quebec? Well, yes, I feel kind of mixed. Sometimes you get so disgusted. It's a really bad thing for Canada. Bad for the eastern provinces. What's going to happen to them? I don't know whether the States would want us or not. Don't like the idea of Quebec pulling out. I don't think they will. I think the idea is 'you give us this, you give us that, or we'll pull out.' Blackmail. I don't think they're that strong. I'd tell them to go straight to hell. I'd fight to keep them in, that'd be the right attitude.''

That's what I think of as the parental view. When a child runs away you get him back. Then, according to your generation you either beat him or you don't then you try to figure out what's wrong with the boy and help him. You don't cure alienation with anger. You cure it with understanding.

"I'm disappointed in Joe Clark. I don't go along with Trudeau's reign, although he's exceedingly smart. Think Wagner would have handled Quebec much better.''

The Major's the oldest provincial riding chairman in Nova Scotia. East Hants riding. "When I took over there was 27 PC votes, 144 Liberals. Wasn't many years before I had a 35 vote majority.'' He's been chairman about 25 years now. I asked how things had changed in his lifetime.

"Change?'' he barked. "We've seen more changes than most. More changes in the sixty years we've been married than in the preceding 2,000 years. For a long time I thought Nova Scotia was stagnating. Biggest move was in 1956 when we elected Stanfield. He put Nova Scotia on the map.''

He stopped for a moment. I kept silent.

"You know,'' he said, "in a way we never had it so good. I've had the poor side too, but we'd be pretty well along with the U.S. with wages and one thing and another. Can't blame the government for that. Labor has pressed too hard, we've priced ourselves out of the market and now we've got lazy and won't work. I wouldn't pass out welfare money or unemployment without making people work for it. Trudeau's turning us into a welfare state. I'd give some [welfare] but not make it a luxury. There's a certain class of people in the middle doing all the work to feed the wealthy and the poor.''

W ELL I SUPPOSE there are men like the major in every province. But I met him in Nova Scotia. I didn't get to Kentville so I never met Victor Cleyle, a man I heard about from an acquaintance at home, but I telephoned him and asked him to tell me about his neighbors and customers.

Victor Cleyle is 43, a native of Kentville, and he operates the men's clothing store his father founded fifty years ago. Ten years ago Victor ran for a seat in the provincial legislature and lost. He's a Liberal, but with one or two reservations.

"The thing that really bothers me," he said, "is that I don't think people here give a damn one way or the other. I don't think anybody believes that the Quebeckers are going to separate. I'm taking it more seriously because I think that these guys are determined idealists. They've decided they'll separate and they'll solve their economic problems later. They'll sacrifice their income, their personal lives, their families, their good name, everything; they're going to bring about separation if it takes them the rest of their lives. And I think they're going to succeed and it's going to be tragic, for them as well as for us. Eventually they'll become Americans. This island we call Quebec is the way it is today only because it's part of a Confederation which guaranteed its existence. That's why I'm so mad.

"What I want to know, and a lot of people are asking this question, is where did the French Canadians ever get the idea they had a right to separate? It's like I decided I don't want to be a Cleyle anymore, it's a legal impossibility. I *am* a Cleyle."

"Well," I asked him, "what if your wife decided she didn't want to be married anymore?"

He laughed. "That's a good question. But where do they get the right to self-determination? Do any of the fifty American states have the legal right to separate from the union? If Minnesota decided tomorrow that they didn't want to be Americans any longer . . . ."

I let him go on for a bit. Victor Cleyle can't change his family but he has the legal right to change his name. The southern states didn't need a legal right to rebel against the Yankees and if they'd won the Civil War the world would have recognized them soon enough. But Victor Cleyle was speaking from his heart and if his legal foundation was shaky his feelings were clear. He's in a peculiar position with the province of

Quebec. He spends a great deal of money there.

"As a retailer I'd say that about 90 per cent of what I buy is from Montreal. More than 90 per cent. Outside of Stanfield's underwear and a little bit of stuff from Toronto, and that's 90 per cent of three quarters of a million bucks and this bothers me because I'm not going to want to buy this stuff from Montreal if they separate."

But he admits he would anyway. He doesn't think Toronto has the men's garment industry that Montreal has. "There was a guy in the store today who said he thinks Lévesque is going to have his cake and eat it too, just like they always have, and this is going to make him mad. That's what he said, 'I'm gonna be madder 'n hell about that'."

Victor Cleyle's father is from Lebanon. He still works in the store and he says he's bilingual and Victor, too. They both speak Arabic. The old man doesn't understand why Quebec can't have her culture, language, cultural institutions and universities and still be part of the whole. Victor, indeed, thinks that is the only way Quebec can hang on to its separate identity. But his father thinks we can solve this dilemma "and I don't, and that's where we differ. I say these guys in Quebec aren't interested in solutions like that."

I asked him if he thought people were more concerned about the economy.

"Oh sure they are," he said. "Unemployment is a real problem and the other, well it's a tragic thing but they don't believe it's going to happen. Unemployment has already happened. You know, there's two kinds of problems. One of them touches people and the other one doesn't."

I asked him about Prime Minister Trudeau and he said "I'm not that turned off with him. Like, I kind of believe that old thing about he's been in power long enough, it's time for a change. But when I look at it as a politician I think we can't let those other guys in, they'll ruin the country for sure . . . and I don't think that traveling road show is helping very much. They're getting the fanatics. The average guy on the street isn't contributing much."

It was time to move on. The CNR runs the ferry service to

Port aux Basques, Newfoundland, and the trains are co-ordinated with it so I went to the railway station to buy a ticket. It would leave at 11:30 the next morning, I was told. Just over ten hours to North Sydney, the ticket clerk told me, and I'd board the ferry there.

"OK," I said, "I want to reserve a berth."

"Fine," he said. "We'll telex North Sydney and you can pay for it there."

"You're sure?" I said, as sternly as I could. "I was told you people handle everything at this end."

"Oh no, sir, we just make the reservations. Don't worry, you'll have plenty of time. The train gets in at 9:45 and the ferry doesn't leave until ten o'clock."

"What if the train's late?"

"Oh, the ferry waits for the train," he said. So I boarded the train the following morning and it moved out into the countryside. I gazed out the window, luxuriating in all that leg room after close to 5,000 knee-cracking miles by bus. You could even get up and go for a walk. Heaven!

There were just a couple of things I hadn't taken into consideration. The general level of efficiency of the CNR, for example. And the sinking of the ferry *William Carson*, just a couple of weeks earlier.

I began to remember the headlines. "ICEBERG SINKS SHIP, ALL 126 SAFE." Then there were conflicting reports. There weren't any icebergs, it must have hit a Russian submarine. "The 351-foot, 8,272 ton Canadian National ferry was plowing through the iceberg-dotted waters off the coast of Labrador when it struck a growler — a submerged iceberg — which pierced its bow . . . ."

Next day a report in the *Globe and Mail*: "No icebergs were visible in the area where the Canadian National ferry *William Carson* sank off the Labrador coast, according to survivors . . . . Survivors also denied reports that they had felt a heavy bump before the call went out to abandon ship . . . ."

Suppose, I thought to myself, that a 351-foot, 8,272 ton ferry sinks. Suppose there aren't all that many ferries serving Newfoundland and Labrador. That might mean there'd be some crowding, right? Not much I could do about it now, though. And the man had *promised* me a berth, hadn't he?

IT WAS A LONG, uneventful but not unpleasant train ride and eventually we pulled into North Sydney; as I got into a taxi I told the driver I wanted to go to the ferry dock. He just nodded. He knew. I waited twenty minutes until he'd rounded up six more passengers — five crammed in the back, three in the front. Then I was lining up in the ferry terminal building and, when it was my turn, I told the man behind the counter my name and said I had a reservation. He handed me a ticket.

"What about the berth?" I asked.

"Sorry sir, the berths are all taken."

"But I made a reservation for one in Halifax." He took my name, flipped through his papers.

"When did you make the reservation?"

"This morning."

"Have to make your reservation a week in advance," he said. "Been busier than hell since the *Carson* went down." I knew it. I'd always known it.

"What about a sleeping chair?"

"They're all gone too, sir."

So I picked up my suitcase and flight bag and headed for the ferry.

Odd, that. Canada is a maritime country. Both west and east coasts must rely on ferry services for the necessities of life, food and milk, for example. But why must people in the Queen Charlotte Islands do without because of political wheeling and dealing? Why must Newfoundlanders depend on a *Scandinavian* company for something as basic as ferries to the mainland which so obviously provide more than holiday excursion services?

It was clearly going to be a long, arduous journey. That didn't matter a great deal to me but it must complicate life for people who live on the island. Surely Confederation was intended to lessen such isolation. And while the sinking of the *William Carson* was unfortunate, why wasn't there a vessel standing by to be diverted? And if the answer is simply that it costs too much, then I wonder why we bothered to annex Newfoundland in the first place. Did we expect Newfoundlanders to prove profitable to the rest of Canada? Or did we want access to fisheries and to Labrador's minerals?

By now it was well after ten o'clock and I'd heard rumors in the waiting room that there would be a considerable delay before departure on the 96-mile voyage to Port aux Basques but I was in a hurry. I had no berth, no sleeping chair and the ship was clearly going to be crammed with people. I reconnoitred the main passenger deck to see what my options were. There was one large room with ranks of chairs which might have been considered luxurious in a movie theatre but were definitely not designed for sleeping. There was a slightly smaller room with the sleeping chairs — long, luxurious contoured seats tilted far enough back that one's head wouldn't fall forward as it tends to do on a bus or train. These were numbered, reserved and — I'd been told — unavailable.

There was a lounge forward and that is where I settled. The bar closed sharp at midnight and when enough people had left I stretched out on one of the upholstered seats. Comfortable but curved, following the contour of the ship's prow, and after a couple of hours I gave it up and went aft, to look at the sleeping chair room. As I suspected, a lot of the chairs were empty so I chose one at the rear and stretched out again, and this time I fell asleep.

I woke up to find someone shaking my knee vigorously. It was a woman and she was annoyed. "Sir," she said, "these seats are reserved and you're in mine."

I blinked a few times and rose, wondering vaguely where to go next. I heard her voice again, seeping through my subconscious to semi-conscious to conscious mind. "But those aren't taken," she said proudly. She was pointing to the whole empty row of seats, one of which had been hers, the one I had "borrowed".

I didn't thank her; I moved, leaving five vacant seats between us in case she had any friends or relations. It was four o'clock in the morning. Never mind. I fell into the vacant chair but I never did get back to sleep. I dozed for brief periods, listening to the snoring that filled the room — it was like trying to sleep in a sawmill.

At 5:30 a.m. I gave up; the day had started. I found a lavatory and splashed water on my face and went to the cafeteria for breakfast, later going outside to watch the approach to Port aux Basques. We docked at 8:30 a.m. and I walked down the gangplank, suitcase in one hand, flight bag over the opposite shoulder, both much heavier than I'd remembered. Small group of people must mean transportation so I joined them. Just one car or station wagon on duty so I had to wait about forty minutes before I got on and was taken to the CN bus terminal.

"When's the next bus for Corner Brook?"

"Just leaving, sir. Full right up. They're getting another one ready and it'll just be a few minutes." The man was wearing a CN uniform so I knew (a) that he must be right and (b) that he must be lying about the time. I went upstairs to another cafeteria and had more coffee, came down and boarded the bus, heaving my luggage on the overhead rack. Oddly enough the bus that was full had been waiting all this time and ours was the first to move. I couldn't figure that out at all.

By now I was tired stupid. This was partly due to the long and virtually sleepless journey from Halifax but it was also an accumulation of fatigue which had been building since Victoria. There had been so many abrupt changes in landscape and lifestyle, and I could see at a glance that Newfoundland would prove the most alien part of the country. There was a curious imbalance to it, the friendly intimacy of the people on the bus contrasting with the harsh land, and I thought it would take far longer than the time I had left to come to know either the island or its people.

An acquaintance in Toronto, a man who had spent a great deal of time in Newfoundland a few years earlier, told me he had experienced this sense of being an outsider. "Newfoundland has never been considered part of the maritime complex," he told me. "They're separate and distant. They have their own language. There was a play at St. John's University, called

'Death Beyond the Grave' and it was a political satire put on by the students. The audience thought it was hilarious and I couldn't understand a line of it.'' Well he had understood enough of it to tell me that one of the skits involved a scheme to row the island south, and to attach it to the United States.

"They have their own imagery," he told me, "and sometimes it's more descriptive. And they have this stoicism. I met a young woman from Burin, one of ten kids in a family, the father disabled. She had no bitterness, just an acceptance of the way things are. There's nothing you can do, it can't be helped — the feeling of hopelessness is built in.''

Another friend of mine, a newspaper reporter who immigrated from Britain, had lived in St. John's in the late 1950s and his wife had given birth to a stillborn child. It was mid-winter and they had little money, and he told me how he and the priest had driven to a cemetery out of town and taken turns digging a grave in the frozen ground. The stoicism had rubbed off on him. It was an appalling story made worse by the matter-of-fact way he told it.

I remembered this as I watched the scruffy pines from the window of the bus. I'd talked to a group of people on the ferry the night before. They'd driven from Toronto to North Sydney non-stop, four of them, and it had taken several days. They did it every year. I asked why, if they were so attached to the island, they had left for Toronto in the first place and one of them looked at me in surprise.

"We couldn't get work at home," he said.

The bus was ancient but the road was smooth and I dozed for awhile, waking up again a few miles outside Corner Brook, the landscape unvarying. But as we came around a corner, suddenly there was a valley and below was Corner Brook, a beautiful sight.

I got out of the bus into a cab and waited. The driver, a woman, was talking to a man, just passing the time of day with no regard for the passenger in the back seat. He turned out to be both her husband and her dispatcher; after about five minutes he gave an affectionate pat to the roof of the cab and the woman turned to me.

"Where to, me son?"

"Glyn Mill Hotel," I said.

"Oh, ye'll never get a room there I don't think. They've got a convention on."

"Let's try it anyway," I said, and we left.

She chattered on in friendly fashion and I responded, trying to rouse myself so the proprietors of the Glyn Mill wouldn't think I was too scruffy.

We arrived at a mansion, a beautiful old building, but there was no sign of a hotel. "Where's the Glyn Mill?" I asked.

"That's it," she said. I asked her to wait for me. If they couldn't put me up maybe they'd be able to tell me who could. So I stiffened my spine, put on a brisk, confident smile, marched up the steps, and crossed the lobby with my last ounces of vigor. As I slapped a Chargex card on the counter, I asked "Can you put me up for the night?"

"Just the one night?"

"Yes, just the one night."

The woman looked through her cards with a dubious expression. My heart sank.

"Yes, sir, we have one room left. Second floor."

"Shower?"

"Oh yes, sir." Salvation. I paid off the cab driver, thanked her for waiting, and took my bags up to the room, which was clean, bright and pleasant and had a nice view out front. Dropped the suitcase and flight bag and went to shut the door. I *thought* I was dreaming and then I realized with sinking heart that I was not. There, marching down the corridor, were maybe five or six devils, scarlet skins, forked tails. Happy housewives in devil costumes: *the convention*. Women's division, rehearsing for the evening dinner. Fun. I closed the door, stripped and stepped into a long, hot shower. Fresh clothing. Then I sat down to consider my condition. Eyes wide open but lids very prickly and painful. Body functioning but awkwardly, knocking ashtrays on the floor, little things like that. I picked up the John D. MacDonald pocket book and started to read and luck was with me; either I hadn't read it before or it was so long ago I'd forgotten. I'd read myself to sleep. It took just forty five minutes and I was ready for bed and I was just rising from the chair when there came a pounding on the door. I opened it.

Harry, the super salesman I'd met in Halifax, had made it to Corner Brook. Harry the super salesman, bristling with energy and high spirits, had just closed another sale. "Come on, we'll go for a walk and I'll show you the town." He beamed at me, positively joyously. "I'll get my jacket," I said. It was about three o'clock in the afternoon. I'd been on the move for more than twenty seven hours.

It was fifty-two degrees Fahrenheit in Corner Brook that day and the wind was blowing something fierce. As we walked, I started to shiver. Harry pointed out the sights and we stopped for a coffee and he spoke to me very seriously.

"John," he said, "you're crazy to take the bus from here to St. John's. You can fly and be there in half an hour."

I looked at him. "Harry," I said, "what's between here and St. John's?"

"Trees."

We stopped at a travel agent's and I bought a one-way ticket for St. John's, leaving about noon the following day. Came outside again and I was shivering uncontrollably. Harry had a customer he wanted to see "for about five minutes." I was to wait for him in a greasy spoon, have a coffee and he'd meet me there. I looked him in the eye. "Harry," I said, "I'm cold and I'm tired and I am not walking back to the hotel."

"No sweat," he said, "we'll hail a cab."

There were no cabs and we walked back to the hotel. It was Friday night and we ate at the hotel, and about eleven o'clock I went to bed, leaving word with the desk to wake me at ten o'clock the next morning, which wasn't necessary.

I was jarred out of a deep sleep next morning by the thunder of hoofbeats in the corridor, as the happy conventioneers pounded on each other's doors. *"Wakey wakey, rise and shine!"* I looked at my watch. It was 6:45 a.m. I wokey, wokey, rose and shone. Clearly Newfoundland was going to kill me.

The plane was only an hour late and by two o'clock I had a room in the Hotel Newfoundland in St. John's, a chicken sandwich and a large glass of milk. It was Saturday afternoon and my plane would take off at about 6:30 p.m. Sunday, carry me to Halifax where I'd board another one that would take me home to Toronto. I had something under thirty-six hours to spend in St. John's, minus sleeping time.

If I'd ignored Harry's advice and taken the bus I would have been in a quandary. The distance, by bus, from Port aux Basques to St. John's is just over 600 miles, meaning at least fifteen hours of travel. It would have taken me close to Dover, a place I'd been hoping to visit, but I'd have had a difficult time actually getting to it. Dover is a small community on Bonavista Bay, where something like 85 per cent of able-bodied men were reportedly out of work, and more than half the residents — including the mayor — were on welfare.

I did pass near Stephenville, on my way to Corner Brook. Joey Smallwood had been premier when it was decided to build a linerboard mill at Stephenville, at a cost of $155 million, mostly from public funds. Construction was followed by four years of operating losses totalling $96 million, a loss to the province of $250 million. At its peak the linerboard mill employed 500 men. They'd closed it down the year before.

Smallwood invested an awful lot of money on grandiose schemes for industrialization of the island, and there's little to show for it now. But Smallwood reminded me of Ed Deibel in northern Ontario, complaining that by shipping raw materials out of the region they were shipping out jobs, too, and therefore their children as well; and they were missing the multiplication of money. Raw materials converted to usable products can generate ten times their original worth. Surely a linerboard mill, converting logs to corrugated cardboard, might be considered a reinforcement of a traditional industry? But it didn't work. I talked with people about the closing of the Stephenville mill but their boundless optimism wouldn't let them believe it was irrevocably closed. There are trees, they reasoned, and therefore the mill will be opened again. Cause and effect.

I hope they're right. I suspect they aren't. Presumably a thriving linerboard mill in Newfoundland would mean losses at an established mainland mill somewhere else. Business tends to look after its own.

I walked through the streets of St. John's aimlessly but bearing downhill toward the harbor. There were half a dozen trawlers with flags I didn't recognize and I watched the crew of one of them playing a form of soccer with a rag-filled ball, cheered by local girlfriends. After awhile I left the harbor and walked again, this time along narrow streets with tightly packed homes rising in tiers above the waterfront, with children playing in torn up roads. The homes had once been painted but the paint had been scoured and the wood was grey. It occurred to me that paint wouldn't last long on the Atlantic coast. I had caught myself equating peeling paint with poverty.

I felt more a stranger, more foreign in Newfoundland than anywhere else I'd been. It was disconcerting and I tried to understand why I felt this way, and what kept coming into my mind was a sense that here, in Newfoundland, the greatest problem is resignation to hardship.

Three different people in the Atlantic provinces — a salesman, an academic and an economist — all told me the same thing: that the people need propaganda to persuade them of their own worth, to give them confidence. Only then could they begin to realize that stagnation is neither deserved nor inevitable, that Ottawa, Central Canada, is vulnerable.

It was the salesman, operating out of New Brunswick but traveling throughout the four provinces, who made the most sense to me. Ottawa's traditional response to a social problem is to pour money into the area, he said, in the hope that the people will be so grateful to get some of their own money back again that they won't notice that nothing has been done about the problem, or at least that they'll shut up about it until after the next election. Politicians have incredibly short time horizons; they can seldom see much beyond the next election.

He told me of an abortive scheme where the federal government had made funds available to a piano manufacturing plant, which had promptly gone bankrupt. Perhaps it happened that way in Stephenville, with the linerboard mill. Inappropriate funding, with no one accountable — not for the honest use of the money but for the *effective* use of the money.

The government would be smarter, he reasoned, to develop a pool of executive talent. "Hire skilled managers on a case-work basis and pay them for success, for results," he said. "Put *them* into the piano factory on a private enterprise basis, backed by government money."

It sounded like a cross between Ayn Rand and American foreign aid but it also sounded like common sense. He had several other things to say.

"Maritimers [he was including Newfoundland] feel they should get a lot more development money. They're kind of forgotten and they're caught geographically. If Quebec goes they're stuck, divided from the rest of Canada."

But it doesn't matter — in this context — whether Quebec goes or not, does it? The Maritimes, according to everything I heard or saw, are already isolated from the rest of Canada. So are the Prairie Provinces; so is British Columbia; so, for heaven's sake, is northern Ontario. Quebec is making noises about sovereignty.

That leaves the people of southern Ontario as the only people in the country who feel at home. That is a disturbing thought.

W ELL I HAD traveled, as closely as I could reckon, some 5,016 miles, from Victoria to St. John's, spanning the half continent I like to think of as my country. I met a lot of people and listened to them as closely as I could, and it was time to go home, time to sort out my feelings about what I'd seen and learned. It seemed to me that the most pertinent comment I had heard came from Jim McNiven in Halifax.

"The real distinction about Canadians," he told me, "is that they're all in little groups — ten, twenty or even thirty — and they cling to these entities very strongly. The Americans had this situation until 1860 and then they thrashed it out in bloody fashion but this country isn't the same. It's too big and too disparate and there aren't enough people in it to have a good civil war.''

EPILOGUE
Taking Guilt-edged Stock

IT IS LATE autumn now. The leaves are off the trees and I can expect the first snowfall any time. I have been sharpening pencils for literally months trying — sometimes sub-consciously, sometimes not — to delay the inevitable con-frontation with that most durable of Canadian institutions, the quest for national identity or its 1970s equivalent, national unity.

It doesn't exist.

It never did.

We are a turbulent marriage but not a failed one and this, perhaps, is our most endearing quality: it is an interesting match. We bicker and squabble and the pedestrian who passes our home is wise to watch for flying crockery. Our neighbors may wish we'd shut up but they're seldom bored and neither are we. Our problems, in this post-liberation period of adjustment, are much in tune with the times.

Here is a Bay Street businessman, stodgy, pretending to be aloof, and married to a grasping, sharp-tongued wench who has decided she will be treated as a lady, as an *equal*. All he wanted was a well-run household, dependable meals, *sub-missiveness*.

He's forgotten why he married her in the first place. She had no money but she'd inherited a lot of property. She was a hard worker and if her religion seemed a bit intrusive she was a damned good cook. All he really wanted was the land. It became a matter of convenience to marry her and by his lights he was generous. He would let her speak her own tongue in her home, and she could follow those of her customs that did not interfere with the prosperity he sought.

He has forgotten that her estranged family is at least as old and proud as his and it amuses him when she draws attention to this. He has forgotten that before her family fell on hard times it claimed practically all the land he didn't own.

Of course he was doing her a considerable favor, saving her from that uncouth huckster to the south, wasn't he? My gracious, he'd even signed a marriage contract with her.

Then one black day she allowed as how the marriage was somewhat less than perfect. He was wounded, shattered. She wanted a divorce. Good heavens, this was unjust. She wanted, however, to keep her land. Preposterous. She wanted to sell him the produce from her land, and at a preferred rate. Now, dammit, the woman has gone too far!

But after all, she pointed out, they had been more than neighbors, hadn't they? They had a special relationship.

I AM NO Nationalist but I am a committed sea-to-sea Canadian. The twentieth century did not, after all, belong to us and thank heavens for that. It belonged to the Americans and very nearly destroyed them. We haven't the wit, wealth or wisdom to rule or dominate the world. If we could, in my lifetime, learn to live together successfully, productively and happily we wouldn't need to. The rest of the world would be pleading with us to teach them the secret.

I'm not interested in us making history so much as thwarting it. And I'm afraid that if the politicians are left to their own devices for very much longer they may do some irreparable harm to our country. It's time for the rest of us to decide what we want, and to persuade our politicians of the need to provide a means of achieving our goals.

The question is no longer whether Canada is coming apart. We have been coming apart for more than a century. In fact, we were never really together.

English Canada is drifting toward self-destruction. That is what I learned from my travels. We'll blame it on René Lévesque if we can, but the fault will be ours. Confederation was never intended to unite Canadians; it was designed to provide a framework and a rationale whereby the Loyalists of Upper Canada, supported by their English-speaking counterparts in Montreal, could exploit and dominate the rest of the country in perpetuity. If the political institutions were democratic, the people in control of them were aristocratic, almost feudal in their outlook.

That is a political truth. Whether it is factual or not (and I think it is) is beside the point. The fact is that a dangerously large number of Canadians from coast to coast accept it as truth and they're fed up. Worse, they've become disillusioned with the idea of Canada, resigned to American dominance and, some of them, even hungry for it. That is an irony of epic proportions, for one of the main incentives behind Confederation was the fear of an American invasion in the west and down the east coast.

Invasion was hardly necessary. Once we'd established our "independence" we were only too eager to give the country away as rapidly as possible. The Yanks own our industries and resources, and through various entertainment and cultural media, our minds as well. Now we're pushing ourselves toward a temporary state of anarchy — Canada East, Canada West and the Sovereign State of Quebec between — which will be even more preposterous than the economic and geographic entity that exists today. Within a decade or two the nation will certainly be annexed by the United States. They don't need or want us. They will feel forced to take us to protect their own security.

That is not a prediction but a projection; it is the direction in which we have aimed ourselves. Nor is it a question of pulling the trigger; the fuse has been lit for some time. It is a question of whether anyone in English Canada will have the wit or will to stamp it out.

I suspect not. We have become too preoccupied with our creature comforts.

It is a gloomy prospect and one I cannot view with detachment or objectivity. If Canada fails then the United States will annex this land and neither partner in Confederation will maintain culture or independence for long. I have no desire to devote the rest of my life to the incessant demands of technology, efficiency and mindless consumerism. Nor have I any interest in exiling myself to that picturesque but bankrupt island that spawned us.

The other night I dined with a friend of mine, a French-speaking journalist who is utterly disenchanted with English Canada but who I think is as committed to Canada as I am. I said to him: "You feel threatened, right? You are a minority of six million people surrounded by 250 million materialistic, technology-happy North Americans, right?"

He agreed.

"Can't you understand that I, too, am a minority?" I asked him. "We are 22 million Canadians dominated by more than ten times as many Americans."

He seemed nonplussed for a moment. Then he looked at me.

"Why," he asked, "did you let it happen? Why don't you do something about it?"

I asked him the question French-speaking Canadians despise us for asking. "What is it you want?" He answered me graciously and, I think, definitively.

"Quebec French. Québécois bilingual."

That is an utterly reasonable position. He recognizes that the people of Quebec must speak English, just as the people of Europe must master other languages if they wish to deal with their continental community. He demands that the intent of Confederation be honored, that French be the natural language of his province. Of course it must. It should have been so long ago. The language bill may cost the province some industries but I am convinced that the French culture is in jeopardy and I demand that it be maintained. If the people are willing to risk some economic disruption then I admire them for it and hope business will adjust. It generally does.

My friend had refused to let me tape the conversation. "If I could speak French to you," he said, "I would not mind. But if I must speak English I do not know how well to have expressed myself." He needn't have worried; he expressed himself very clearly. Even my Icelandic friends in Gimli, Manitoba, would have little difficulty with an attitude as eminently reasonable as his. It is not threatening. It is constitutionally correct. It is inoffensive, in fact reassuring; I would grieve to see the anglicization of Quebec just as I would grieve to see French-speaking Canadians outside Quebec forced to choose between home and culture. Better for all French-speaking Canadians to have two homes — their own and Quebec.

He gave me some small ground for hope. I do not believe that René Lévesque has a mandate to lead his people out of Confederation, I think he won his election by default. He was the only apparent alternative to Bourassa. But — again, a political truth — he *believes* he has such a mandate, and therein lies the danger. We in English-speaking Canada could frighten Quebec into supporting him, partly through insensitive bumbling in Ottawa, partly by over-reacting in what could be construed as a bigoted manner among ourselves. We are capable of extremely bad political judgment. Twice in my own lifetime we have elected messiahs to save us, then sneered and scoffed at their inability to do so, forgetting the fact that it is we who need saving. In a world of hawks and doves, bulldogs, bears and dragons, we thought we were beavers and perhaps, for a time, we were. Now we are mere lemmings embarked on a fatal pilgrimage to the sea.

For a while last summer I thought our newspaper editors at least had come to their senses. There was a period of perhaps four or six weeks when our disastrous economy had pretty well wiped national unity stories off page one.

The problem is that national unity is a gutsy story, exciting and fluid but somewhat misleading. If we could solve our economic problems, deal effectively with the regional disparities that turn us against one another, I firmly believe we could resolve the question of national unity in a week. I said resolve the question, not answer it; that might take longer.

That is what I believe people were telling me as I crossed the continent, that if Confederation was simply a matter of concentrating the wealth of the country in Central Canada then perhaps the East and West would be better off on their own or as part of the United States. The problem as far as newspapers are concerned is that the real crises we face are extremely complex, difficult to write about and boring to read — economics, pollution, unemployment, welfare, regional disparities.

Arguing about national unity is like riding a roller coaster. It's exciting because it gives the illusion of danger without the reality. But this particular roller coaster is a decrepit and rickety contraption whose timbers are rotting and unrepaired. Inevitably it will one day collapse and there will be an awful tragedy; people will wring their hands and say they don't understand how the authorities could permit such a terrible thing. What they will not do is demand that the thing be shut down for repairs, and dirty their hands ripping out the rot to restore their plaything so they can live to enjoy the illusion of danger, secure in the knowledge that it is safe to do so, for the next 110 years.

So we would have to stop riding the roller coaster for a while, to inspect our constitution, our political institutions and to replace what needs to be replaced, if we were to decide we wanted to continue to enjoy the land. It would be dull, dirty work, very expensive and far more of a threat to our complacence than the Parti Québécois will ever be, for we'd have to confront our injustices and be prepared to correct them and that would involve a profound change. The Péquistes are not asking *us* to change but simply to let *them* do so, since we clearly don't wish to.

But if I heard the people right, then the Péquistes are simply our most visible or audible minority and the first to rebel. There is a dreadful sameness to the complaints I heard all over the country. They focused on unemployment and inequality, jobs and money. That is why I think we may well be doomed. It's one thing to die for your country. It's quite another matter to spend a dollar to save it, or — most terrible of heresies — to take a modest cut in pay, a small drop in our standard of living, in order to ensure that all Canadians live well and benefit from being Canadians.

What can we do for our country? Many things, most of them painful, many of them costly, all of them essential if we would survive. And many of them are inevitable even if we don't. If we let Canada slip between our fingers the problems of the prairie farmer, western lumberman or fisherman, eastern miner or Ontario factory worker will not disappear. The colors of the flag may change but the color of coal or wheat will not. Nor will distance dwindle, nor mountains flatten, nor polar icecap melt. It's easy to see what we stand to lose if we let the country go, but I can't for the life of me see what we'll gain. Different masters but not better. Different problems but not lesser.

Where to begin?

Redistribution was as good a place as any.

It was difficult to argue with Doug Christie, in Victoria, or with the myth that representation in the House of Commons had something to do with population. From his office in Victoria, where he runs a law practice as well as the fledgling Committee for Western Independence, Christie pointed out that on any rational basis the west was under-represented.

This has been changed, and high time. For many years Central Canada has dominated the nation and the extremities have suffered. British Columbia, aside from distance, travel and transportation costs and the inevitable sense of isolation caused by the looming mountains, has had little political clout. They have had to subsidize central Ontario. They have had to pay heavy freight costs for goods that come from the East when their neighbors in Seattle were importing the same goods from the Pacific Rim countries and paying much lower prices. Automobiles from Japan, for example. We don't permit them to do that without paying heavy tariffs, up to $600 per car.

That is supposed to protect the automotive industry in Canada, which just happens to be located in Ontario.

And anyway, it doesn't work. Our automobile trade deficit with the United States in 1975 was $1.9 billion.

Which is more important to me, as a Canadian: maintaining an automobile industry in southern Ontario or knocking $600 off the price of a Datsun in Vancouver? I can't answer that question and I shouldn't have to. With proper representation in Ottawa, British Columbia can achieve a fair settlement, correct any inequities.

Surely it is a basic of any democratic society that representation in parliament should be directly related to population? Redistribution is a beginning. But there are a number of questions we must consider. Some of them have to do with regional disparities, others with the whole concept of Canada, what it means in real and physical terms, what it means in philosophical or political terms. The questions are complicated and, many of them, unanswerable and yet they must be considered. Having considered them we must find ways of communicating our answers (or our confusions) to each other and to our politicians.

Who owns the oil and gas in Alberta? Prime Minister Trudeau has answered that one for us, most emphatically. The oil and gas belong not to the people of Alberta but to the people of Canada. Thus Alberta must sell its rapidly diminishing fossil fuels to the rest of Canada at a price far below that the Americans would pay. But Alberta has only twenty or thirty years of oil and gas left. Which is more useful to me, cheap heating for my home or a vibrant, powerful and versatile industry in Alberta twenty years from now? I think that I'd have to say the latter. If Alberta, when its resources run dry, has to return to an agricultural economy based on the uncertainties of wheat, I'm going to suffer one way or another. If, by paying more for my heating, more for automobile gasoline, I can help Alberta become industrialized and economically self-sufficient, why then it would almost be an investment, wouldn't it?

Not really. Thirty years from now I'll be in my seventies, collecting my pension and complaining about the injustices inflicted on people with fixed incomes. The only beneficiaries of my farsightedness today will be my children. Do I really want to pay $2 a gallon for automobile gasoline to benefit my children thirty years from now? Yes and no. If I answer yes, it will be more for my country than my children and yes, I guess I owe my country that much.

But is it true, as Ed Diebel says in North Bay, that we are exporting industrial jobs to the United States, to *Norway* every time we ship a pellet of iron ore out of the country? And we permit this in direct contravention of the Ontario Mining Act? That's absurd. It's criminal. It's true. Then why should I pay a single cent more than I have to for Alberta fuel when my own government won't enforce one of its laws to help industrialize northern Ontario? Diebel says that six million tons of iron ore leave Thunder Bay for U.S. smelters. Surely that's enough for a smelter of our own? The same is true of pulp and paper products. We don't make paper in northern Ontario, we only make pulp, and presumably we only do that because pulp is easier to ship than logs.

There are just over 800,000 people in northern Ontario, Diebel tells me, while there are sufficient resources to support three or four million people. Meanwhile three things are happening. First, we are exporting jobs and wealth to the United States. Second, four million Canadians are living below the poverty level in Canada and young people in northern Ontario have to leave home when they finish school and move south if they want jobs. Third, we are paving rich agricultural land in southern Ontario because it's worth more as parking lots and industrial sites than it is as farmland. But what are we going to eat? And there are areas in the north which fairly beg to be industrialized. You can't grow radishes or apples on rock but you could make steel there, and probably buy all the coal you need from Saskatchewan. Suppose we did that, paid the world market price for oil, bought coal from Saskatchewan and manufactured steel (and newsprint) in northern Ontario. Three sections of Canada would be strengthened and our gross national product would rise. Young people would no longer have to leave their homes. Is that simplistic? I am neither politician nor economist, but does that mean I'm stupid? Well it's either me or the politicians, because it doesn't add up. Why would I sell you my apples if I could make ten times as much by baking them into apple pies and selling them? You'd have to be holding a gun to my head.

Why do I want to industrialize the north? That's easy. I'd like to cut down on poverty, strengthen my country, reduce the number of have-not provinces and increase the number of haves. Back in the 1950s we used to call it "enlightened self-interest" but the phrase has gone out of use. Why do I want to industrialize Canada? I don't, really, I just want to strengthen the country. I want to do that partly for the sake of the people who live here, partly to prevent us from being totally overwhelmed by the Americans.

I don't despise the Americans. I just think they've let their technology get out of control. Americans exist to serve their economy, by consuming. Perhaps we still have a chance, being underdeveloped (compared to the U.S.) to preserve a different set of values with more emphasis placed on the quality of life than simple affluence. We accomplish nothing by giving our wealth away.

These are the questions we should be asking ourselves, those of us who want Canada to survive. How important is the nation and how much are we willing to sacrifice to keep it intact? Suppose that the federal government announces a scheme for redistribution. That should take the wind out of the sails of a lot of alienated westerners. Suppose Queen's Park decided to enforce the Ontario Mining Act. Suppose Ottawa announced some sort of compensation for Alberta, something that Peter Lougheed could use to diversify the province's economy. Suppose other people put forth ideas to restore our confidence in our own government. English-speaking Canada would then be putting its house in order with some legitimate optimism. Optimistic people — equipped with jobs or the prospect of jobs and armed with honest representation in Parliament — aren't going to have quite as large a chip on their shoulders.

Then we could deal with René Lévesque.

I met René Lévesque once, in a priceless confrontation. I was a cub reporter for the *Telegram* and I'd been sent up to the CFTO studio in Agincourt to interview him. When I found him, smocked up in the make-up room and looking even more absurd than usual, I asked him whether he thought the recent mailbox bombings in Westmount had done his movement any good. I suppose it was a dumb question but I don't like terrorism and I did (and still do) like René Lévesque and thought it would give him a chance to divorce himself from such tactics and, simultaneously, give me a punchy *Telegram*-style lead: "René Lévesque denounced terrorist tactics in an exclusive *Telegram* interview today, although he stood firm on his separatist philosophy . . ."

Instead he spun round, his make-up smock flaring like a cloak, and pointed angrily to the door. "This interview is *over!*" he shouted, enraged. "Get out!"

I shrugged my shoulders and pocketed pad and pencil and began to leave, but I hadn't crossed half the floor before he called, still angry: "Come back here." Apparently space in the *Telegram* was not to be ignored no matter how abrasive the reporter. My recollection — after fifteen years — is that the interview got printed more or less as planned but I can't be sure; it was a long time ago.

Prime Minister Trudeau, once a crony, now describes Lévesque as an enemy who is good for Canada because he is making Canadians think about their country. "He knows he is the enemy of Canada such as it is constituted now . . . I think it may be a good thing for Canada that a man of Mr. Lévesque's stature is forcing Quebeckers and Canadians to make up their minds."

The problem with that is that we seem to be in danger of being emotionally stampeded and losing our sense of direction. Already there are signs of over-reaction. If we permit ourselves to become polarized along racial lines we are doomed as a nation, and we will most certainly terrify those French-speaking people who live outside Quebec.

History is fascinating stuff and can be of great comfort in time of war but has, I think, little to offer politics. For various historical reasons, Quebec has been subjugated, confined, held back. The reasons are interesting and not very flattering, either to French or English, and should be left alone. History tends to kindle passions and right now at least one side must remain dispassionate, concentrate on the present and the future.

The only historical aspect that seems valid or relevant to us today is that when the English defeated the French on the Plains of Abraham they decided, wisely and in the Roman tradition, to be magnanimous (if exploitive) and to guarantee certain cultural rights to the conquered people. This was not, I suspect, done from a purely altruistic point of view. It is one thing to win a battle but quite another to change an entire culture. Much cheaper to persuade that culture to accept a different situation and to make common cause with the conquerors or, perhaps more accurately, with the victors. The French were never conquered, simply defeated in battle.

This led, ultimately, to the British North America Act, recognizing Quebec as an equal partner in a contract. If we renege on that contract today, the first time it is seriously put to the test, then our original purpose is lost and we have little to offer nationhood that the Americans (or the Parti Québécois, for that matter) can't improve on.

We can no more afford to police a reconquered and hostile Quebec (if it could, in fact, be reconquered) than our ancestors could, nor should we want to try. A forced marriage or reconciliation is useless today. If we would achieve a reconciliation then I suppose we must first demonstrate that the contract is both valid and effective. Then we can settle down to the urgently needed constitutional reform. It can't be done as a response to blackmail from either side.

That is why the reactionary events in Essex County and Cavan Township upset me; such occurrences, though unimportant in themselves, tend to cloud the important issues with emotionalism and unnecessary polarization. In a real crisis — and this *is* a real crisis — we need all our wits about us. We have to convince ourselves that all Canadians benefit from being part of a unified Canada. Since this is rather difficult to do, given the divisions that have arisen across the country, we must attempt an even more difficult task, that of persuading each other that we intend to change and improve our nationhood in the immediate future. And that is something better done with action than speeches and statements of intent.

Yes, the prime minister's description of Lévesque as a beneficial enemy and politician of great stature certainly applies. Lévesque has finally demonstrated the urgency of our situation and has caused me to think very closely about Canada, what it means to me, what I am prepared to sacrifice to maintain it. But I don't know whether I have the wisdom or the time to find a workable solution. Thus the beneficial enemy may simply make us more keenly aware of loss. It is an uncomfortable position and I wish that we had been more sensitive, more farsighted. Certainly there were plenty of warning signals.

We are currently involved in civil war. Perhaps we can demonstrate to the world that guns are outdated, that civil wars can be fought to a just end without them. That would be no small contribution for Canada to make to civilization. It would also strengthen our hand, for we would also be demonstrating to ourselves and to the world that we have something worth preserving. It is, perhaps, a small moment in world affairs but it has the potential for greatness.

So far we have left the battle to politicians and academics. The mass of Canadians — and according to a summer poll conducted by the Canadian Press this applies to Quebec as well as the rest of us — is preoccupied with survival: jobs. Oddly enough, both the Liberal Government in Ottawa and the provincial Conservatives at Queen's Park would prefer to talk about national unity than the economy, while opposition parties at both levels of government keep hammering away at jobs.

Opposition leader Joe Clark says Canadians are tired of the national unity issue. "More and more Canadians are recognizing that the problems of unity are not confined to Quebec," he said in September. Last summer NDP leader Ed Broadbent told a party convention in Winnipeg that providing jobs is the key to unity. "To make Canada work as a nation is to put the nation back to work," he said, adding that it's no wonder Quebec is disillusioned with Confederation. "Quebec has a quarter of our population," he said, "but a third of our unemployment." It was the beginning of his "third option" program emphasizing jobs and fairer government rather than major constitutional change.

Ontario Opposition Leader Stuart Smith, writing in the *Toronto Star*, observed that "our country is not simply an economic unit, but it cannot long survive as an independent state in the shadow of the United States unless we have a successful economy . . . . If concrete steps and effective leadership are taken in the economic area, then I believe Canadians will be prepared to examine arguments for constitutional change with a commitment that the effort of preserving the nation is, in fact, worthwhile . . . . We are currently experiencing not only the crisis posed by the possibility of Quebec separation, but also severe regional alienation felt in Atlantic Canada and in the West. Our institutions must evolve if we are to deal effectively with this sense of alienation . . . ."

Meanwhile the federally appointed Task Force on National Unity — a traveling road show starring John Robarts and Jean-Luc Pepin — has attracted fairly meager audiences, although the people who have attended the hearings have had much to say. Pepin observed at one time that Canadians are indulging in "a colossal game of passing the buck" and Robarts observed that dealing with national unity "is like trying to shovel fog."

Does the poor attendance reflect public disinterest or disillusionment? Either way I find it disturbing and not very surprising. During my own travels I found few people talking about national unity. Sometimes if I brought the subject up I might get some pungent comment but mostly people were concerned with jobs and prices, isolation and alienation.

Ottawa's response has been hardly less reassuring. First there was the battle of statistics, with the federal bureaucracy claiming that Quebec profits from Confederation and the Quebec provincial bureaucracy claiming the reverse. Then there was the federal decision to spend $13.6 million on films, exhibits and various national unity projects including a traveling exhibition on bilingualism. Well, at least $13.6 million ought to generate a few jobs.

Little good can come of two bureaucracies attempting to demolish each other with statistics. Bad enough that we let our politicians do battle for us; if we rely on civil servants we haven't a hope.

Two conferences were held in Toronto, both on national unity, one by York University and the other by the University of Toronto; countless essays are being published in magazines and newspapers but there are few letters to the editors from people at large. Forty-six English-speaking academics and writers signed a manifesto in the summer issue of the *Canadian Forum* magazine, claiming that they "do not believe that Canada without Quebec must break up into weak fragments to be inevitably absorbed into the United States."

It was a useful document and the conferences were useful too, but it seems that most of the dialogue is being conducted either by politicians or by people who, one way or another, make their living by thinking about such things and articulating the various points of view. It would be more reassuring to hear people talking about the issues at the bus stop level. That is where pressure for change and flexibility must come from if it is to have any real validity.

Certainly there is a lack of leadership in English-speaking Canada (although no dearth of candidates) but real leaders are hard to find. They are the people who listen to us all, determine what we want and show us how to achieve our goals.

Relying on paid thinkers is dangerous because although they do our thinking for us, they have no particular incentive to listen. I fear that we are drifting deeper and deeper into divisiveness and disinterest, and that we may wake up one morning — as we did in November, 1976, when Lévesque was elected — to find we have drifted into something irrevocable, something we didn't really want. The *Canadian Forum* manifesto (it was attributed to the Committee for a New Constitution) is a case in point. Its authors claim that absorption by the United States isn't inevitable (which is quite wrong, of course) simply because Quebec decides to withdraw from Confederation, and that we should be prepared to bargain from a position of confidence and strength, if that should come to pass.

It's theoretically true. There are many smaller nations than Canada in the world, although none with such an impressive imbalance between territory claimed and population. But if we let Quebec opt out through inertia rather than through a collective decision, then will we also lose our will to survive?

That was what disturbed me most during my Canadian odyssey. People were so preoccupied with their own affairs and problems, so isolated and insulated from each other in spirit as well as geography that it occurred to me that we have already made our decision, by refusing to make a commitment.

In LATE 1967 I asked an American friend what he thought Canada might celebrate, what we had to be proud of, during the Centennial year.

"Survival," he said. "Isn't that enough?"

It's taken me eleven years to come up with an answer.

"It's nice, but no, it's not enough. We've got to do something better than anyone else in the world has ever done," I should have said. "And the only thing we can afford to try is living together."

Yeah, I should have said that.